COMPLETE CONFIDENCE

Also by Sheenah Hankin, Ph. D.

Succeeding with Difficult Clients
(with Dr. Richard Wessler and Dr. Jonathan Stern)

COMPLETE CONFIDENCE

A HANDBOOK

SHEENAH HANKIN, Ph.D.

10 ReganBooks
Celebrating Ten Bestselling Years
An Imprint of HarperCollins*Publishers*

This book contains advice and information relating to health care. It is not intended to replace medical advice and should be used to supplement rather than replace regular care by your doctor. It is recommended that you seek your physician's advice before embarking on any medical program or treatment. All efforts have been made to assure the accuracy of the information contained in this book as of the date of publication. The publisher and the author disclaim liability for any medical outcomes that may occur as a result of applying the methods suggested in this book.

A hardcover edition of this book was published in 2004 by ReganBooks, an imprint of HarperCollins Publishers.

HarperCollins books may be purchased for educational, business, or sales promotional use. For information please write: Special Markets Department, HarperCollins Publishers Inc., 10 East 53rd Street, New York, NY 10022.

FIRST PAPERBACK EDITION PUBLISHED 2005.

Designed by Kris Tobiassen

Hand illustration by Adam Walko

The Library of Congress has cataloged the hardcover edition as follows:

Hankin, Sheenah.
    Complete confidence : playing the game of life with a winning hand / Sheenah Hankin.
       p. cm.
    Includes index.
    ISBN 0-06-009647-0 (alk. paper)
    1. Self-confidence. 2. Self-actualization (Psychology) I. Title.

BF575.S39H39 2004
158.1—dc22

2004041785

ISBN 0-06-009650-0 (pbk.)

06 07 08 09 WBC/RRD 10 9 8 7 6 5 4 3 2

In loving memory of my brother,
Peter John MacKenzie, 1947–1996

CONTENTS

COMPLETE
CONFIDENCE

ONE

CONFIDENCE: THE PATH TO FREEDOM

To be confident a person must walk a path to freedom, arriving at a place called Emotional Maturity. The people you will meet there are competent, high achievers. Cheerful and calm, they are free of anxiety and depression. They will welcome you, for they are not shy. When annoyed, they will set a good example with their straightforward honesty. They play the game of life with a Winning Hand, and you can join them if you make the journey.

The path to Emotional Maturity can free up everyone's inborn, natural confidence. Like any journey, there is much to gain and some necessary losses. On this pathway to confidence you will discover new ways of thinking and acting, and gain the emotional management skills that are the bedrock of complete confidence.

What you will lose are the immature emotions of childhood and adolescence. Fears of judgment and correction will be gone. There will be no more shaming self-criticism, and no helpless self-pity, for confident people are self-reliant and rarely need help. Instead of feeling guilt about not pleasing other people or resentment about having to please them, you will listen to yourself and do only what you believe to be right and necessary. And to further lighten the burden of emotional immaturity, you'll learn to calm and comfort emotions internally, within the brain, ending dependence on binges and addictions, the insecurity blankets so many people cling to.

"But Sheenah," you might ask (my clients call me by my first name and I hope you will, too), "this is some promise you are making. Is it mere psychobabble?" Good question. Let me answer it. Notice how you are dissuading rather than encouraging yourself to try. Realize how your doubts about our confidence project are built on dark predictions of disappointment and failure. If you see success as unlikely or even impossible, you undermine your confidence.

Begin now by fighting against any tendency that will undermine your effort. "This won't work." "I've tried before and failed." "This book is probably just the same old self-help stuff." "People can't change." These ideas are self-defeating, and in a way self-pitying and humiliating. You are not so powerless.

Instead, listen to the opportunity knocking at your door right now. It's not the sweepstakes guy ready to hand you a check for a million dollars. This is an opportunity that doesn't require any luck or good fortune. The Winning Hand knocks on your door. I stand waiting with my hand outstretched to take yours and walk forward into confidence and success. Confidence is worth more than a million dollars, so make the effort for yourself.

Hold out your hands and marvel at how much they do for you. They protect you when you fall. They feed you. They hold the hands of those you love. They massage, caress, and arouse. They wave good-bye.

You have a hand in your own troubles, too. So, as you hold your hands in front of you, look hard at your fingers. They can also poke and point in criticism and accusation at others and yourself.

The mission of this book is to enable you to take yourself in hand.

I can help you gain the confidence you need to retire your Losing Hand. Playing with a Winning Hand means you will activate every talent you have, eagerly take every opportunity you are given, and calmly solve every problem you face.

It is time to stop blaming yourself and others, to stop pointing a finger at the flaws you falsely perceive as preventing you from living a successful life, to stop generating shame and self-pity. It is time to give up the habits of a loser, and to think and act like a winner.

PARTNERS IN CONFIDENCE

Partners starting a business sign a contract. As my future partner, please read this contract carefully before you sign it.

"But Sheenah," you ask, "why should I trust you? I haven't even met you." If you want to know more about me before signing the contract, first read the next section. I hope you will then agree to be my partner in confidence.

The Commitment to Confidence Contract

1. I will read *Complete Confidence* from beginning to end.

2. I will practice all the strategies and behaviors that are required for a confident life, and repeat them over and over again so that I can learn to become confident. (People learn by rehearsal.)

3. I will be very persistent because it is not intelligence, money, or good luck that leads to success; it is persistence.

4. I will have faith that I can learn to be more confident. I will not listen to my feelings if they make me feel that I will fail.

5. I will begin to read *Complete Confidence* today and I will set time aside every day until I finish it—I will not put off this project.

I commit to the aforementioned conditions:

_____

Your Signature/Date

I, Sheenah Hankin, commit to being your partner. I promise that the methods I describe in my book work when you fulfill your commitment, which I trust that you will.

Your partner:

Sheenah Hankin
_____
Sheenah Hankin

MEET SHEENAH, YOUR PARTNER IN CONFIDENCE

Unlike therapists who reveal nothing about themselves, I prefer the openness of self-disclosure. So, I'll tell you a little about myself. In my busy practice in New York, I invite every client to ask me personal questions, for people are usually curious about shrinks. What are their private lives like? Are they secretly nuts like those depicted in the movies and on television? Do they have children? How do their children and marriages turn out? Are they obsessed with sex? Are they competent and confident? Do they have enough professional and real-life experience to be helpful?

I decided to begin as if you were my new client and this is our first session. What's different is that before I begin to try to explain you to you, I'll try to give you a feel for what my life was and is like. I will begin with a terrifying moment that for the first time pointed out to me that I could not expect anyone to take care of me. I alone would have to do it, and care for my four children, too. When my perfect life skidded to a terrifying halt I knew of only one solution. If I had enough money I could glue it back together, and the cracks would never show.

My life looked like a preppy fashion commercial. A tall, dark-tanned, fun-loving husband, four small, handsome sons—and I, a stick-slim blond wife. We glistened with affluence.

It honestly never crossed my mind that after fifteen years of marriage, this ordinary day would be different from any other. It began as usual. I heard the baby stir very early. Reluctantly I crept out of my warm bed, sensing the damp chill of a drizzly Irish morning.

Passing a window on the way to the nursery, I noticed a low sky and a silver pall of fog setting in over the Irish Sea. It misted the trees in the old established gardens with a croquet lawn and ancient hedges that enclosed our large home in fashionable County Wicklow.

I prepared oatmeal as usual for my older boys, but it was not their footsteps coming sleepily down the stairs of our grand staircase that I heard, but the heavier step of my husband. "I don't know how to tell you this," he said. "We have lost most of our capital." We, I thought. What the hell did I have to do with it? It's his fault.

My husband came from a family who lived large. My father-in-law was a self-made man. He created a fortune and he spent it. Big houses, big boats, big swimming pools, and bigger parties were his style. I had never experienced this in my suburban, puritanical Scottish family. So, after I married, I lived it, I loved it, and I came to expect it.

Yearning to become a successful entrepreneur just like his father, who had died from excessive drinking, my husband frittered away his considerable inheritance on investment gambles, wild ventures, and failed businesses. I would have no part in his financial affairs. I knew I was smart intellectually, and I had a fine education. The Scots are big on education, but my father and mother were both clueless when it came to money, and I knew nothing. It was his money, anyway, I believed.

Who was I to suggest that maybe we should buy something solid, like houses, and rent them out? What did I know? It was my husband's job to take care of me, wasn't it? So, I kept quiet, and I kept busy raising four sons and arranging ladies' lunches, with a touch of charity work thrown in. Women's work.

At first I could not accept the truth. My brain fogged up with fear and anger, and then I exploded into a rage that had been building up for years. I blamed everyone and everything: my husband, the stock market, our stockbroker, my crazy in-laws, and eventually my mother. Notice that I left myself off the list.

My mother taught me that if a wife supported her husband emotionally, then he would support her financially. It's what she had done. My father was a brilliant design engineer, but a lousy businessman and a tyrannical husband and father. We all cowered in fear of his rage. Fortunately, he worked unceasingly, so we had the beanstalk to ourselves until the giant's footsteps were heard at the door. I used to tremble and hide as soon as he turned the door handle. My mother cooked, drank coffee with other wives, and accepted his hostility without comment or criticism. In fact, she praised him. "He's so clever. He loves you so much," she would tell me. As a young girl I walked around in my mother's high heels. As a young woman I copied her beliefs and emotions.

Who would take care of me now? And how on earth could I take care of my children? I stood there, weeping and yelling just like my two-year-old. A helpless woman: I was healthy, intelligent, educated, lively of spirit, creative—but had absolutely no confidence. Like everyone else who undermines their own confidence, I eventually turned on myself. "You loser. You stupid loser. What will your friends think of you now? Why did you rely on a man to take care of you? Weren't you a feminist in college? When did you give up your values and your ideals? You weren't a partner in this marriage, just another dependent child. Why did you listen to your mother?"

The crisis killed off a marriage that had been dying for years. I don't know how I ever found the courage to leave. Like many young women with kids and no confidence, I ran home to live with Mummy, who was widowed. She welcomed her grandsons into her large messy house, but she was quietly livid with me. Women must be loyal, she reminded me—I should go back to my husband.

My mother delivered her message in subtle ways. In effect, I became her housekeeper, earning my keep by cleaning and cooking, and accompanying her to boring charity events where I served tea and coffee to the ladies. Mother never let me get comfortable. If I were uncomfortable enough, she thought, maybe I would go back to my husband. She even went as far as inviting him for Christmas, without asking me, to make her point even more clearly, but we could not play happy family for her.

I yearned for my own life—a cheap car, a tiny house. I walked down the side streets of the small English town where I grew up, past rows of run-down Victorian cottages. I dreamed of fixing them up with pretty wallpaper, a flower garden, and a warm fire for the boys after school. Who would give me what I wanted? I had vowed never to marry again, so the only person I could turn to was me—self-critical, depressed, whiny old me. A woman of no value—that's what I was, in my opinion. I was expert at blaming myself for my pathetic life.

I considered going back to school, but the very idea of university terrified me. I had spent my undergraduate years at the University of Birmingham in a constant state of anxiety. I had struggled with what I now know was depression. I had missed classes, procrastinated, and fallen so behind in my work that I felt too ashamed to attend lectures. I was so self-conscious that I could not eat in the university dining hall, because the boys would look at me. Did they think I was fat, I worried, or was I a sexy slut? I hid in the library in utter misery, feeling safe behind the books I felt too dumb to understand.

The pompous, ivy-covered buildings filled with me dread. It is as if the Victorians poured all the passion and sexuality that they dared not let into their lives into these soaring, complex buildings. The only passion I felt was a desire to run away. I didn't want to return to a place where I had felt like such a loser.

Rather than hide once more in the library, I scuttled across town to a modern glass and concrete skyscraper, the University of Aston. A new beginning seemed possible. No professor from my past would see me and know that the loser was back. I could be anonymous, and my shame would go underground in this new territory.

Aston offered a course in counseling and psychotherapy, a unique program, open to only a few highly qualified mature students. I badly needed counseling myself, even though on the surface I managed to seem cheerful and confident. I could feel waves of anxiety well up and my chest tighten as I walked into the office of Dr. W. Dryden, a sharp-tongued young man with a fierce stare, who was chewing on his pipe. "Sorry," he said flatly. "The course is full; you are months too late to apply." It was early June. I pleaded and begged. Mistaking my desperation for enthusiasm, he relented, "Call me on September fourth. Maybe someone will drop out." On September 4, at 9:00 am I dropped in. "You are lucky. We have just one place open. The cost is . . ."

"I have no money," I told him. I had nothing in my purse but three pounds and a train ticket back to my mother's house. "What?" he said, "You expect to get a graduate grant, too?" "Well, it's that or the welfare rolls," I replied. He hurled an application at me. I filled it out and received a grant that covered my tuition and left me barely enough for the five of us to live on. I never received a penny in child support from my husband.

I entered graduate school feeling stupid and incompetent. I was desperate to get qualified and work so that I could take care of my sons, but I wondered how on earth I would cope. It was clear to me that my boys needed new shoes, not a mother who was a shattered wreck. I worked hard in the quiet of the very early morning, the only time I had away from caring for my mother and my sons. My course work soon began to make sense to me. I learned to speak up in class, to feel more competent, to succeed and have fun. I was on my way.

Two startling moments during this time helped me to see things differently from the way I had when I entered the program. I was late with an important term paper, because my sons and I were sick with the flu. Dr. Dryden's policy was: be on time or your paper will not be read. Surely, he would make an exception. "No way," he said. "You want to be a counselor, you have to be responsible and show up for your clients on time. You have an F." Internally furious, I hoped that this evil, rigid martinet would be struck down with some long-lingering disease.

I stormed out of his office, ran to a window at the end of an empty corridor, and hugged the warm radiator. I stared hopelessly at the glass office buildings set against the gray industrial sky. It was drizzling and I was weeping. Poor me, another guy had refused to understand my plight and take care of me. As I calmed down and brought my emotions under control, the clouds in my head cleared. I made a life-changing decision. I would forever stop blaming myself and others for life's reversals.

I decided that blaming the boss for keeping the rules was a dumb idea. Another dumb idea was transferring the blame to myself. In the past I would have called myself a stupid loser who procrastinates about everything. Now I saw this setback as a very helpful experience. It resulted in a promise to myself to become an extremely reliable person, and I've kept that promise. I always show up and on time. I keep the promises I make to myself, and I will keep the promises I make to you.

My revelation that day was just the beginning of my personal crusade for confidence. The second startling moment involved a man on the university faculty to whom I was attracted. I was in fantasyland about him, yet in his presence I acted like a fourteen-year-old. I was awkward, sarcastic, anxious, and embarrassed. Even though I had no evidence, I assumed that he thought I was a stupid, ugly loser. I also knew I couldn't stand these feelings.

I began to change them, again as a result of something Dr. Dryden said. We were required to demonstrate our counseling skills in front of the whole group. We all trembled at the prospect. "Why do you care so much what others think of you?" he asked us. "Give it up." My mother had given me the opposite advice. She was a classic pleaser. She taught me that it was wrong to upset others and to get angry. "If you can't say anything nice, don't say anything at all," was her advice. So for years I had held in both my opinions and my feelings.

This policy of passive pleasing had clearly failed me. I would try a new approach. I refused to care what the guy I had a crush on thought of me. If he rejected me, so what? I would survive. I openly flirted with him, and he responded. The flirtation lasted a few months, and I felt like a woman again. I realized that I was not a dependent drudge no man would want.

I moved back to Ireland and taught the biology program at my sons' school. I bartered teaching for their school fees and a rent-free apartment. I found a counseling job and built a private practice that paid our bills. I shocked myself one day when I reached into my jacket pocket and pulled out a bunch of Irish pound notes a client had paid me. I had forgotten about the money, but I will never forget what it felt like to be debt-free and have extra cash that was not spoken for.

I regret one thing only. I had announced to everyone who asked that I would not marry again. I advise my newly divorced clients never to make this prediction. One day at a training workshop, I met Richard Wessler. I had loved his recent book. Over time, I found it was just as easy to love the man himself, and we decided to move the family to the United States. I started over; I married again, but this time I was confident. Soon I had a practice and an income, but most of all I had lost my fears. I can handle others' criticism. I can stand my ground. I encourage myself to take appropriate chances and I can calm my feelings.

Sometimes I stand outside my lovely Victorian house on a tree-lined street on Manhattan's Upper East Side, and I ask myself, "How did that scared young woman who lacked the confidence to even imagine taking care of herself, get everything she once could only dream of?" I could have sunk into dependent, miserable middle age, nursing my resentful mother and comforting myself with too much food and alcohol. But I didn't. When I was forced to make a choice, I chose confidence. You can, too.

I have spent many years working with clients and struggling to understand why so many of them are playing the game of life with a Losing Hand, as I once had. By now, I have helped hundreds of people turn their lives around, as I have mine. I invite you to begin now by making a very serious commitment. However before you commit, let me be frank and clear about what you are committing to. You are committing to developing a radically new understanding of yourself.

You will discover how you habitually re-create feelings of shame and self-pity. In turn, these feelings generate anger, anxiety, and depression, plus the self-defeating thoughts and behaviors that erode and destroy your confidence. You are committing to learning how to change these habits. You are committing to confidence. Please sign the Confidence Contract if you have not already done so.

A CONFIDENT BEGINNING: WHY I WROTE THIS BOOK

It happened in Madrid about five years ago. I was feeling trapped, sitting in the architecturally mind-blowing lecture hall of the Spanish College of Surgeons between a couple of intense young guys with steel-rimmed glasses, goatees, and serious expressions of the graduate school kind. To be frank, I only attended this particular presentation to show support for my friend, who was chairing this early morning symposium. He had gone missing. His well-documented partying habit had resulted in his sleeping through the whole meeting. His abandoned colleagues on the panel shuffled their speeches and themselves.

Eventually, one chap rose to his feet and decided to make the best of the situation. He acknowledged the absence of the chairman, but offered no explanation or speculation. He began his paper. Ever optimistic in a British take-a-cold-shower-it's-good-for-you way, I listened. Maybe he would have something to offer me—some ideas to take home to New York and help me improve as a therapist—you know, some enlightening new invention or intervention. It was not to be.

He started to drone on and was so obviously nervous that we all grew nervous, too. I thought how undronelike he was: a slightly balding fellow in a short-sleeved, button-down shirt with rapidly spreading damp patches under each arm. Real drones are high-flying, sexy fellows who spend their short lives buzzing about doing nothing whatsoever except trying to score.

In my profession of psychotherapy and counseling there have always been mentors of the moment. I, the good student, had always tried to be open to new trends. I do not mean to say that I did not get something from each of these ideas. But on this day I sensed a psychological epiphany: an end to my postgraduate-student dependence on others to be right and to know the way.

I love my work, and I am as dedicated and tenacious as Sherlock Holmes. For twenty years I have been seeking the answers to certain mysteries: Why are so many people who seem to have everything they want still so unhappy? Why do people who could, with effort, have everything they want fall short, based on their belief that they somehow could not achieve it or don't deserve to? For example, why is TV so stuffed with ads for useless weight-loss products, but people are reportedly getting fatter? You must have seen the one with the before and after guy holding up his old elephantine, sofa-size pants and proclaiming that confidence grows as your waistline shrinks.

What is behind the epidemic of upsetting emotions that lead to more and more ads for antidepressants and anti-anxiety medications? Most people don't need them, and those who do, need them only for a matter of a few months. These drugs will certainly damp down your disorderly emotions, but are very likely to damp down everything else over time. Memory, for one thing, and your interest "down there," as my mother whispered on the only occasion I can remember her ever acknowledging that she or anyone else had private parts. Yes, they can damp us down, down there, too. We won't miss it, but it can make us very unpopular with those who love us. Luckily, the urge grows back when the pills wear off.

Meanwhile, time was dragging in Madrid. My neighbor had nodded off, and he jerked awake as I snuck out of the lecture hall, blinded for a second by the sudden flood of intense sunlight, but stone-cold clear in my mind about what I would do next. I ran and broke into a dance step or two along the wide tree-lined boulevard toward the gates of the Prado art museum, absorbed in my freedom and my new plan. Eventually, I became aware of the funny looks I was getting from passersby: What's wrong with this señora, jigging and muttering to herself, and what's written on that large plastic badge pinned on her? Psychology something? How did she escape from the locked ward of the psychiatric institute for the eternally nervous?

What they did not know was that I felt like Archimedes in a dress. "Eureka!" cues were going off in my brain. Eureka! I would never go to another ditch-dry psychological conference ever again. I felt just like I did on the last day of high school.

Eureka! Instead of being talked to, I would take the floor. I would help my clients to understand how their immature emotional habits eat away at their confidence and self-respect. I would show them what to look for and what to do to grow up. I so relish the difference that confidence has brought to my life. I know how free it makes me feel. My approach works, and it can help a lot more people than I could ever see in my office, which is why I decided on that Spanish morning to write this book.

I had described the approach in a book I had just coauthored and published with Richard Wessler, my husband and also my partner, and with my close and valued associate, Jonathan Stern. The book, *Succeeding with Difficult Clients: Applications of Cognitive Appraisal*

Therapy, was written for mental health professionals. The enthusiastic response it received was inspiring. However, books like this can expect only a small readership. Now I wanted to reach the public at large with this approach. It will take you far less time than it took me to stop being a follower and become a leader in your own life. So, let's continue to work together.

TWO

YOUR FEELINGS ARE THE PROBLEM

n the beginning we are all emotion. New parents often tell me how they wish their newborn had arrived with a precise list of directions, like a VCR or a cell phone. But babies give their own directions. Their immature brains cannot make rational decisions, and they can't even see straight yet, but their emotional demands are loudly voiced. "Take care of me, *now*" is the clear message in their first pitiful, guilt-inspiring cry.

All babies are born to become confident. I would love to tie an imaginary label with a pretty pink or blue ribbon around every newborn's tiny toe with these instructions: "Help this child learn to manage his or her emotions and behavior. Help this child to exercise self-regulation. Give this child a set of sound personal rules for living on which to base his or her decisions as he or she grows up."

I have one more set of wishes for parents: that they raise their children to be confident, so that as adults they are free from worry except in the face of real-life threats, which seldom occur; that they can speak openly without fear of censure or offense; and that they are able, on the rare occasions when faced with real hardship and loss, to react calmly, positively, and confidently to the challenges that troubling times bring.

The confident among us see the world as manageable and see themselves as competent and therefore likely to succeed. Immature feelings of anxiety, anger, guilt, shame, and self-pity do not haunt them. When faced with difficulties, they do not blame themselves, others, life, or God. They do not feel sorry for themselves. They play life's game with what I call a Winning Hand.

If everyone were confident, I would gladly pursue another line of work, and I think it is a good goal for anyone who reads my book to try to put me out of business. Confidence requires mature management of our actions and interactions with others. In order to live this way we must manage our feelings. The good news is that if this training was absent or incomplete in our upbringing, we can still raise ourselves to be confident, and we can still free ourselves from the immature and troubling emotions of childhood.

Let's be frank: Our immature feelings make far more trouble for us than the troubles we will face.

Let's be clear: Most of the time in our daily lives, nothing much happens *to* us.

The ability to overcome our immature emotional responses and calm them down quickly separates confident people, who play life's game with a Winning Hand, from those who do not. Have you ever met parents who told you how they are actively training their children to manage their emotions? I haven't. Did you know that children have, and should have, very different emotional reactions to life than adults? I certainly didn't, and I wish I had had this information when my four fine sons were just small boys.

As a young adult I had the emotional habits of a child, and I was certainly playing with a Losing Hand. I could have fooled you had you met me then, for I was quite sociable and charming and nervously chatty, but I did not fool myself. I yearned to have you like me and strove to please you. I feared your criticism as a dark and dangerous force that had the power to destroy what vestige of confidence I had. Fear of criticism hung out in my mind like a stealth missile, ready to strike at any time. When life's setbacks and reversals, which I once called mistakes and failures, came my way and I was held accountable, I adopted a childish defense mode. I would blame something or someone else. Later, in the privacy of my own brain, I turned the firepower of shame on myself and felt like a stupid loser.

I have held the hands of many people with a habit of self-criticism. They blamed themselves when things went wrong and, unable to tolerate criticism from others, responded with immature outbursts of blame, rage, and sulking. Just as I once did, many felt like victims in a world they unquestioningly saw as dangerous, and lived in a state of anxiety, busily obsessing about how they were going to be victimized in the future. They told me of their fears: rejection, scorn, and betrayal; accidents to loved ones or to themselves; financial rip-offs; jealous predictions of infidelity; and various creative dark fantasies of impending doom and even death. Believing worry to be an insurance policy against disaster, their days were stressful and difficult, and their nights were restless and exhausting.

Too much worry wearies the brain, which expends the same amount of energy on anxiety as marathon runners or professional athletes do on physical challenges. Worriers can expect no winner's T-shirt, let alone a contract worth millions. They are handicapped by stress and fatigue, losing energy that could have been used to promote survival, success, and a sense of their own well-being and of the world at large.

It took me many years of working as a full time psychotherapist to find the answers to why people repeatedly undermine their confidence and to marvel at how expert I was at undermining my own. In my early years of practice I grew puzzled and frustrated. Yes, I had passed all my exams and, honestly, excelled in graduate school, but many of the clients who were unfortunate enough to sit opposite me simply made little or no progress. There were some people whom I doubted I could really help to change, and I felt guilty taking their money.

My training had been a necessary and essential beginning, but it did not help me to understand this puzzling mystery: Why would anyone want to stay with miserable feelings and in miserable situations when they had a choice not to? And why was I so critical of myself? I was practicing what I was taught and doing my best. It must be my stupidity, I thought.

In a strange way it was reassuring to discover, after a lot of reading, thinking, and discussing, that others in my field did not have the answer, either. But what helped me most—and it took years—was criticism and conflict. Every night, on the hour-long drive from New York City to our home in the suburbs, I would argue, often loudly, with my husband, Richard, a brilliant psychologist and psychotherapist. He would challenge every new insight I had, just as he challenged his colleagues and graduate students. Other couples fight about money and the kids, and we did our share of that, too, but mostly we fought about why people do what they don't want to do, and why they seek help but seem reluctant to change. Here is an example of me proving my point:

RICHARD: Why would people have feelings that are not rational? You need some proof. You can't just "know it."

SHEENAH: Their irrational feelings are familiar. You know, "familiar," from family, from their family upbringing.

RICHARD: Are you saying that their feelings define them, and give them a sense of security, even if they don't make sense? Are you telling me that people seek bad feelings without knowing it? This will get you in trouble. For the past century, psychologists have taught that people only seek pleasure and avoid pain, and here you are saying that people also seek painful feelings and avoid happiness. You'll meet a lot of opposition in our field.

SHEENAH: Of course. Psychologists, like everyone else, feel secure by sticking to what is familiar. That's just my point.

RICHARD: Is shame all there is? What about the self-pity you speak about, and have plenty of, in my opinion?

SHEENAH: I think you do, too.

RICHARD: That hurt.

SHEENAH: "Hurt" is another way of saying "self-pity."

RICHARD: I don't get it. No one wants to be a self-pitier. No one would proudly announce, "I feel sorry for myself."

SHEENAH: But we feel sorry for ourselves when we get criticized—and get mad, too.

RICHARD: Good point. You're right about that. Many of my clients feel weak, helpless, and angry. They're so afraid of criticism and disapproval that they don't stand up for themselves.

SHEENAH: Yes, they feel victimized.

Through experience I came to see that each and every one of the clients who sought help and had tried self-help only to slip back into their own self-defeating ways lacked the same essential quality: confidence. Feelings blur commonsense thinking. There is a secure and familiar ring to the beliefs many clients state about themselves when I first meet them. "I am an anxious person." "I have a gene for depression." "I cannot stand conflict." These absolute self-descriptions are based on immature feelings, not reality. They color our trust in ourselves and deny us our inborn human ability to be both courageous and adaptable to change.

Let's be frank: Life isn't difficult. Our feelings make it feel that way.

Let's be clear: The confident life is the only life worth living.

EMOTIONAL IMMATURITY EXPLAINED

Unless we are raised in an environment that provides us with the opportunity to become independent and emotionally mature, we will look like adults and in many ways act like adults, but we will lack mature emotional habits. Children are often scared and anxious. If left alone, a small child will feel very uneasy and panicky.

Children feel ashamed when they fail to please their parents—and they should. They also fear punitive consequences for what they do wrong—and they should.

Children have no real power. A family that includes small children is not a democracy. Parents are loving despots—and they should be. As a result, children strive to get more power by trying to make their parents feel guilty: "It's not fair," they say, "my friend's dad lets him do it." Or, "You're stupid, Mommy." They should fail in their attempts to gain power through guilt. Children naturally express anger in an immature way. They cry, they rage, and they sulk. In these ways they will try to guilt-trip their "leaders" (their parents) to comply with their wishes. This should also fail.

Temper tantrums are yet another dramatic production designed, however unconsciously, to bully the audience into compliance. They can also be mounted as revenge against the powerful parents who will not comply with their children's wishes. Parents should not respond by feeling guilty and indulging a child's whims.

Instead, parents or those in authority should calm and comfort children's dramatic painful feelings, either immediately or following a penalty period for poor performance. Our brain is not designed to function in an ongoing state of high alert. Unless calmed and comforted, it will protectively shut itself down into a depressive state. Children whose distress goes unattended will stem their chemical lava flow of burning feelings—they will withdraw and feel helpless, hopeless, and depressed. This shouldn't happen.

An overcriticized child will come to criticize him or herself, creat-

ing shame and sparks of self-pity and anger. A child who feels victimized is angry at those who thwart him or her. Disconnected from the
protection of a parent's love, a child is seriously anxious and feels
abandoned. Any criticism will, to some extent, have this effect on children, all of whom are constantly scanning their environment to check:
Am I okay? Is anyone mad at me? Is anything wrong with my caretak-
ers? Can they take care of me? This is as it should be.

A mature person does not overreact to criticism and does not fear
abandonment. Confident that they can protect and care for themselves, they know that their world is calm and secure. They know that
most of the time nothing much happens. Mature adults are also confident about self-respect. Shame is not a problem for them, for they do
not fear criticism. They do what they believe to be right at any moment in time, not what others tell them, and so they have no need to
criticize and shame themselves.

They do not complain and cry. They know that their environment
will *not* give them special attention. They do not believe that the bus
should be on time for them, or that bank lines should be short when
they need cash. They are not enraged when people accidentally bump
into them. The waiter does not have to pay them immediate attention,
and the haircut or color the beautician gives them may not turn out exactly like that shown in the movie star's picture in a magazine.

They never use phrases like:

- It's not fair.
- I can't believe it.
- What's the world coming to?
- It's not like the old days.
- The waiter is a lazy bum.
- The beautician should be fired.
- I can't stand these long lines.
- It's crazy to expect me to have to put up with it.
- Life sucks.

- He is stupid.
- She is stupid.

They do not see the world as an efficient utopia designed to anticipate their wishes and service them. Do you meet a lot of these confident people? I don't, and I expect you don't, either. For too many years I was a self-pitying complainer who would attempt to guilt-trip others into meeting my demands. If this failed, I would shame them—behind their backs, of course; I was too fearful of being criticized to be honest and open.

I remember when I was a younger mother, I would often act as emotionally immature as my kids. The four small boys in the back of my car would start up almost as soon as I started the car. "How far is it? Do we have to go? Are we there yet? I'm thirsty. Are we there yet?" I would take it for a while, and then they would start to quarrel and fight. I would pull over and scream at them, "It's not fair! Stop! Shut up!" Then we would all yell and cry, everyone blaming everyone else.

I was physically capable of taking care of my sons, but I was certainly emotionally immature, and I did not know it. I would overreact. I could not calm them down because I could not calm myself down. It wasn't very British—a little more stiff upper lip would have been useful, but I was acting on self-pity and rage, not reason. I was as immaturely intolerant, self-pitying, and enraged as my four small sons.

The immature are not in control of themselves. They lack the confidence that commands respect and, unlike confident people, treat others disrespectfully when angry. Confident people do not have tantrums or sulks. They express anger calmly and without blaming themselves or others. They are not anxious, because they do not have to live in fear of being victimized or humiliated in the future. They do not feel powerless and sorry for themselves, because confidence in their abilities provides great energy for solving life's normal reversals normally. They are in control. When emotionally mature people experience hot flashes of immature, emotional overreactions, they do not rely on others or on substances to calm them. They can do this all by themselves. People who lack the confidence to play life's game with a Winning Hand all have some degree of E.I. (Emotional Immaturity).

Let's be frank: Life's normal reversals require normal mature responses.

Let's be clear: Emotional Immaturity is not a disease or a disorder—everyone can mature.

EMOTIONAL IMMATURITY: A SUMMARY

Emotional Immaturity is apparent in anyone who has an overload of feelings, from too much anger immaturely expressed—the sulkers and the ragers; to too much anxiety immaturely expressed—the worriers, the procrastinators, and the avoiders. E.I. is obvious in those who are immensely self-critical—the shamers; you can spot them easily because they criticize others a lot, too. You can easily detect E.I. in those self-pitying complainers who claim that life is difficult and that no one cares but them. E.I. is present in all the depressive fortune-tellers who predict that bad things will happen in the future.

Listen carefully to anyone who tells you that they are depressed. Emotionally mature people may become very sad when they experience trauma or loss, and the sadness may linger, but they do not get depressed. The majority of depressed people have E.I. They feel helpless and hopeless, ashamed and sorry for themselves. Depression is so often a catchall diagnosis given to people with an E.I. problem. An emotionally overloaded brain will react by shutting you down, in an attempt to calm you down. Your brain becomes depressed. It demotivates, it slows down, and in extreme cases, it immobilizes the stressed person.

THE EMOTIONAL MATURITY QUIZ

There is a clear and noticeable difference between confident people, who manage emotions maturely, and those who lack confidence and are emotionally immature.

Here is a quiz to see if you are emotionally immature.

Anger:

1. Do you get angry easily?
2. Do you get angry several times a day?
3. Do you regularly have trouble sleeping?
4. Do you regularly wake up in a bad mood?
5. Do you lose your temper?
6. Do you sulk?
7. Do you feel easily insulted?
8. Do you find fault with yourself when others are angry with you?
9. Do you resent authority?
10. Are you rebellious and contrary?

If you answer yes to any of the above, Emotional Immaturity is damaging your confidence. You are not yet playing life's game with a Winning Hand. Mature people feel angry occasionally, when they are disrespected or disadvantaged by someone or some event in their lives. They respond honestly and calmly, and do not blame anyone or anything. Their anger passes quickly.

Now let's take a similar quiz to check to see if you manage anxiety immaturely.

Anxiety:

1. Do you often feel nervous?
2. Do you often have a shaky, anxious feeling in your chest?
3. Do you often get butterflies in your stomach?
4. Do you fear that something bad will happen to you in the future?

5. Do you constantly check to make sure everything is in order?
6. Do you worry about being embarrassed?
7. Do you get anxious when the phone rings or the mail arrives in case you might be in trouble?
8. Are you scared of things when there is no rational reason for this fear (for example, public speaking, flying, social events, disappointing others)?
9. Do you have a phobia that stops you from doing what you want?
10. Do you feel that others might judge you to be stupid, fat, old, ugly, or a loser?

If you answered yes to any of the above, you lack confidence and are not playing life's game with a Winning Hand. Mature people feel anxious occasionally in response to a real threat, not just a felt threat. They react by taking protective action, calmly. They do not live in fear, and they can calm themselves down. Their anxiety passes quickly.

People who lack confidence easily feel anxious and angry. If someone close to you regularly gets angry or anxious for reasons that make no sense to you, you can now see that they are emotionally immature, and need a copy of *Complete Confidence*'s prescription for calm and confidence.

DON'T TRUST YOUR FEELINGS

I long wondered why feelings are so often seen as positive and valuable, and are honored as healthy guides to the real self. Decisions based on feelings alone usually turn out badly. Feelings are real enough, but what feels true may not fit the facts. People in the grip of a frightening panic attack often believe, falsely, that they are dying of a heart attack. The fact is, their overstressed, overloaded brain is supercharged with jumbled feelings, and subject to temporary confusion—electrical impulses that will soon sort themselves out.

Depressed people feel as if their future is one of dark hopelessness.

They are often deeply ashamed of their inability to function, due to their helpless feelings. The fact is, even without treatment most people who are clinically depressed will recover after a few agonizing months. Then, the world feels once again as it was before their emotions took over their reason. Their future brightens.

People who are highly anxious feel like helpless victims in a dangerous world. They startle easily, and their traumatized nervous systems jolt rapidly into a fearful state. Those who are anxious *over*react to real threats. Worse still, they are anxious about their fantasies, their "what if the worst happens" focus. They believe their fears, and frighten others with doom-laden reminders, such as, "The world is in the worst state it has ever been in." "Really?" I respond, listening to their anxious emotions and carefully avoiding a meaningless discussion based on what their feelings tell them is true.

I often tease my clients with a sinister story about myself. "If I had trusted my feelings," I tell them, "I would have killed all of my children." Like a horror movie, this is a fabrication, a moral fable, but I confess that it contains a grain of truth. When I managed my immature and histrionic anger less well than I do today, and when I felt sorry for myself because I blamed my children for having caused more work for me than I believed they should have, I felt hostile and had thoughts as to how to punish them. But I did not. My reason prevailed.

Let's be frank: Do not trust your feelings. They will lead you astray.

Let's be clear: Do not trust anyone who advises you to trust your feelings.

"But Sheenah, do you think we should all act like Mr. Spock in *Star Trek*, and make decisions based only on logic? That makes no sense. Why do we have feelings if we shouldn't act on them?" Let me remind you that Mr. Spock was half Vulcan and half human and all fiction. Every decision we humans make has an element of emotion in it. Let me describe the nature of emotions and their purpose.

Anger explained: Anger, like all our emotions, has a serious purpose in everyone's life. Anger is a *reactive* emotion. We react with anger when we do not get what we want, or when we don't want what we get. What we want can be logical: a pay raise, a good haircut, or good service in a store or restaurant. What we want can be psychological, too. We feel sorry for ourselves and angry if we are not given the raise; ashamed and angry if we must live with an ugly haircut; ashamed, sorry for ourselves, and angry if our waiter treats us with a couldn't-care-less attitude—perhaps we are too insignificant to warrant his attention.

Anxiety explained: Anxiety, which is a popular name for fear, also has a very serious purpose in everyone's life. My mother would describe the anxiety she felt during World War II. As the evening darkened into night, baying sirens would awaken her. Trembling in fear, she would wrap herself in a comforter and run to the bomb shelter to huddle with her neighbors, anxiously listening to distant explosions. Her fear and anxiety were reactions to a real danger. My mother also had psychological fears. She wanted to have a baby, but was too anxious. She feared that her child could be hurt, imprisoned, or even killed by a future enemy.

The purpose of anger is to make us powerful. It motivates us to actively insist that we get our needs met. It motivates others to fear us, and give us what we want. It comes on fast. *The purpose of anxiety is to warn us.* Like a smoke alarm, when anxiety sounds we rush to protect ourselves by escaping, or if this is not possible, by freezing, hoping to be unnoticed. Anxiety or fear sets in very fast.

Shame explained: The purpose of the more chronic and deep-seated feeling of shame is to remind us that we need to keep ourselves in check. Shame can be a permanent feeling that stews internally. "Are we acceptable? Will others reject us?" At a primitive level, lack of others' acceptance could stop them from coming to our aid in an hour of need. This causes us to fear rejection, because on rare occasions, just as children do, we need the help of others in order to survive.

Self-pity explained: Self-pity is the other chronic, deep-seated feeling. We feel sorry for ourselves if we feel powerless or victimized. We need assistance. We cry and complain so that others will feel guilty and pay attention to our plight. In this way we can inspire guilt in others.

Guilt is a version of shame. We only survive because we are family folk. We help each other. We are not loners like the great white shark or the tiger, which never need support once they are mature. We feel guilty if we act inhumanely, or fail to feel sorry for and assist the weak and helpless. This may cause shame. The victims who are denied our support get sorry for themselves and angry, and inspire us to feel more guilt and shame. To avoid these feelings, we come to their aid.

Reactive feelings—anger and anxiety—occur rapidly to make us aware of our environment.

Anger—the power tool in our emotional tool kit. We use it to fight off an external threat. We blame, we threaten, and we attack when we fear that we will be deprived or our survival is threatened. Alternatively, we silently stew with resentment, and plot revenge.

Anxiety (fear)—the alarm system in our emotional tool kit. It instantly warns us to take evasive action when we perceive that we are going to be deprived or victimized, and our survival is threatened.

Chronic feelings—shame, self-pity, and guilt—persist to make us aware of who we are.

Shame—the measuring tape in our emotional tool kit. We measure our acceptability, our power, and our importance. If we believe that we do not measure up, we perceive that our survival is threatened, and we blame ourselves and feel ashamed.

Self-pity—the cell phone in our emotional kit. Feeling helpless, weak, and needy, we call to others for help and comfort by expressing our misery. If others refuse to help us, we feel afraid for our survival. We will blame them first for victimizing us and then for not responding to our pleas.

Guilt—the remote control in our emotional tool kit. It turns us on to the potential shame we will feel if we harm other people or do not respond to their needy self-pity. If we tune into their channel and watch out for them, we can avoid shame.

To help you be clear, I have summarized on the following chart five emotional habits that damage confidence.

Five Immature Emotional Habits

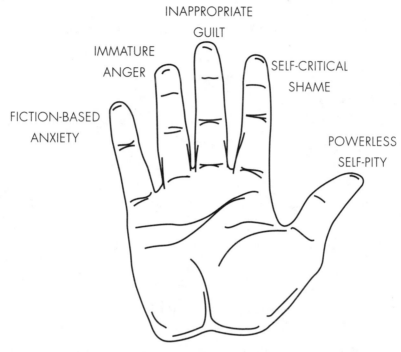

INAPPROPRIATE
GUILT

IMMATURE
ANGER

SELF-CRITICAL
SHAME

FICTION-BASED
ANXIETY

POWERLESS
SELF-PITY

FICTION-BASED ANXIETY:	IMMATURE ANGER:	INAPPROPRIATE GUILT:	SELF-CRITICAL SHAME:	POWERLESS SELF-PITY:
Fear of non-dangerous threats. All phobias. Fear of criticism and conflict. Social avoidance. Procrastination. Perfectionism. Unproductive worrying. Calamitous predictions of the future. (See chapter 9.)	Rages. Threats and insults. Sulks. Blames others, the world, or God. Blames self, even when clearly not at fault. Passive-aggressive actions (revenge through indirect punishment, e.g., avoiding sex). (See chapter 8.)	Feels guilty having done nothing wrong. Feels guilty and apologizes when others are angry or upset. Pleases and complies with others to avoid feeling guilty. Induces guilt in others for one's own ends.	Labels oneself as stupid, fat, old, ugly, and/or a loser. Blames self when things go wrong. Refuses to believe compliments or accept praise. Compares self with others to "prove" self to be a loser.	Feels helpless and overly sensitive to criticism. Sees others as unfair or uncaring. Fears future events. Exaggerates difficulty of tasks. Fears and dislikes authority. Binges. Prone to crying and complaining.

Let's be frank: It is a good idea to understand your feelings.

Let's be clear: It is a terrible idea to automatically act on your feelings.

WHEN IMMATURE FEELINGS DAMAGE CONFIDENCE

"But Sheenah, I still don't quite get it. I now understand what my feelings are for and how they protect me. So, how do they become problems that damage confidence?"

Experience gained from over two decades of full-time private practice has convinced me that almost everyone I have ever helped suffers from a painful case of *Emotional Immaturity*. To emote, think, and act in a childlike manner in a mature world is to be handicapped. It is a condition often mislabeled as a lack of self-esteem. I know it as a lack of confidence.

You see, there is a difference between confidence and self-esteem. Self-esteem is based on positive affirmations, even a policy of self-love. It assumes that one has an internal nanny who lives to tell you that you are cute, wonderful, lovable, and smart, just because you are you. In adults this unearned approval is believed to be a magical cure for the self-critical disapproval so many heap on themselves. Like antibiotics, jolting the system with doses of love will not prevent the next shame virus from spreading its infectious message of criticism.

Confidence is very different. The confident recognize the immature, shameful, and self-critical feelings, as well as the childlike self-pitying helplessness so many adults feel. These feelings are met as a serious challenge, and then modified with calm and comfort. With practice they cease to be influential, freeing a confident person to pay attention to others and the world, and not be governed by feelings like children. The Winning Hand of Comfort (chapter 7) will show you precisely how to achieve this.

A young client of mine was the daughter of two emotionally immature parents. They were both hippies who never grew up or settled down. They lived a marginal, peripatetic life. My client never had regular meals at normal times. There was no bedtime, and sometime no bed. There was no discipline and little instruction as to how to live in a group. Unused to the mature world, she was too scared to eat in public or have a meal in a restaurant. She could not calm herself without drugs. "I wasn't raised," she told me. "I don't know how to act around other people. I don't fit in and I cry a lot. I need a boyfriend to take care of me. I don't structure my life very well. I'm twenty-five, but still a kid."

She is an extreme example of a woman with an Emotional Immaturity problem. I gave her some good news right away: Anyone can mature—that kind of change is normal. If you suffer from Emotional Immaturity, you can mature, too. Your immature feelings are roadblocks to a path to confidence, so you need to become more emotionally mature. Together we will achieve that.

FEELINGS AND PHYSICAL ILLNESS

Feelings can cause physical problems, too. Work time is lost, relationships strained, and creativity stymied as a result. If I eat too much, I, like you, will feel sick and maybe even throw up. If I feel too much negative emotion too much of the time, I will feel sick, too. I will stress my immune system, for feelings, like food, are biochemical, and too much emotion stresses my stomach and my system. Like a vicious hangover following an alcoholic binge, prolonged overloaded emotional states cause negative physical symptoms in the body. Here are some of the problems they cause or contribute to:

- Anxiety attacks
- Full-blown panic attacks
- Hyperventilation
- Agoraphobia (fear of being in a place perceived as unsafe)
- Hypochondria

- Posttraumatic stress disorder
- Irritable bowel syndrome
- Sexual dysfunction (inability to achieve orgasm or to maintain erections without true medical diagnoses)
- Connective tissue disorder
- Migraine headaches
- Chronic fatigue syndrome
- Tinnitus (ringing in the ear)
- Some asthmatic problems
- All psychosomatic disorders, including bad backs, muscle pains, neck pain
- Severe and prolonged PMS (worse for women who cannot manage feelings)
- Dermatological problems (hives and skin eruptions)

CHECK YOUR CONFIDENCE

It doesn't take long for me to know that a person has too little confidence. I listen for certain key statements I have heard many times before. Here is a partial list. If you recognize yourself in one or more of these statements, this book is for you.

- I am always afraid that others will think the worst of me. I am such a wimp. I try to please others rather than voice my own opinion. I get anxious whenever my boss or someone in authority asks me a question, even when I know the answer. And I don't like myself for not speaking up, for being so weak and nervous.
- My body is ugly. Whenever I look in the mirror, all I see is my fat stomach and dimpled thighs, etc. (fill in your own body parts). I wonder if my partner is as turned off by my body as I am. I know I should lose weight, but I can't stick to any diet for more than a few days.

- I am a binger. If it's in the fridge or the cabinet, I eat it. All of it.
- I feel like a fraud. Others tell me I'm successful, but I know that I'm just lucky. Compliments make me uncomfortable.
- I have a problem with commitments. I quickly find fault with everyone I date and yearn to be with people who are not interested in me. I am so lonely, and I feel frustrated because I can't understand why I'm like this.
- I procrastinate and leave things to the last minute. I try to start something only to immediately distract myself with trivial chores like cleaning the kitchen or organizing my desk. I don't know why I do this to myself.
- I'm such a perfectionist. I drive myself crazy trying to complete my daily "to do" list and it just gets longer.
- I want to get off antidepressant medication, but I don't think I can manage without it.
- I don't sleep well. My mind spins and I worry about all my past and potential mistakes. Sometimes I don't sleep much at all.
- I am too old to change. It's pointless to believe I can make up for all those missed opportunities I was too frightened to take advantage of in the past.
- I don't like crowds or parties. I don't like small talk. I don't know how to keep a conversation going. I feel like a loser.
- I dread hearing the telephone ring. I screen my calls. I know it will be bad news, or someone yelling at me for doing or not doing something.
- I was an underachiever in school. Nothing's changed. I know I am smart in some ways, but somehow I stop myself from doing as well as I can. I feel stuck.
- I have the worst taste in men (or women). Everyone I date turns out to have serious problems, but I don't realize it until it's too late, and then I don't want to let go. I don't want to be alone.
- I either have a tough time maintaining an erection or I climax too fast. I am afraid I can never satisfy a woman.

- I rarely climax. I'm afraid he won't be satisfied unless I have an orgasm.
- I have a good life. I love my family and my work. It makes no sense that I feel so unstable and depressed so much of the time.

Did you find yourself on the list? The statements that apply to you will generate feelings of anxiety, anger, guilt, shame, and even helpless self-pity. These feelings are not based on facts, but on your own very familiar fictions—your stories about yourself. They may feel like reality, but they are mostly just ways to create trouble for yourself and to keep you hopelessly stuck.

Let's be frank: Do not trust these feelings.

Let's be clear: Expect to further damage your confidence if you do.

If you act on fiction-based feelings, you create more reasons and excuses for not changing how you think and feel about yourself, and for maintaining your habitual patterns of thinking, feeling, and behavior.

THE CONFIDENCE MYSTERY

The following statements show people's inability to understand why they get stuck in feelings and habits they would love to change, but do not. See how well you understand yourself. Ask yourself the same questions I ask my clients:

- Why do you seek perfection?
- Why do you fear criticism?
- Why do you procrastinate?
- Why not stop bingeing?
- Why are you so shy?
- Why are others' opinions of you are so important?
- Why are you so very self-critical?

Are you puzzled by these questions? Or do you respond the way so many people have—with knee-jerk excuses and generalizations:

- "I don't know why—I try to change but I eventually slip back."
- "That's me; it's my nature. It's who I am."
- "I'm too depressed to change."
- "I've always been shy. I'm a shy person."

Instead, I hope you will say, "Sheenah, I never really understood the reason why. How interesting. Can you tell me right away so that I can change?" I will be glad to tell you, but first let's solve the puzzle of why people are reluctant to change even after I let them know the reason.

FEARING CHANGE

You have heard lottery winners say, "I'm not going to change a thing. I won't give up my job. No new house, either. I'm staying right here." Or the abused child who begs to go home to the abusive parent. Or those battered spouses who frustrate their friends and counselors by ignoring good advice and staying with abusive partners.

Major life changes—good or bad—cause anxiety. Our first response to the fear of the unknown is to stay with what is familiar to us. Just as we feel safe at home, so, too, do we feel safe with familiar feelings.

Let's be frank: People seek the security of familiarity more than they seek happiness.

Let's be clear: Your familiar negative feelings undermine your confidence.

There is no true security in sticking only to what you are used to, because change is inevitable. New experiences cause every one of us to change. However, it's also natural and normal for us to seek security. We will often discount reality (for example, a positive compliment, an opinion about us we do not share, even an exciting opportunity we don't feel up to), if it doesn't fit with the psychological picture we have of ourselves. The way we judge and feel about ourselves, even if it is negative, feels real and secure. Most of us get locked into a box called The Self, and can't think outside of it. No college degree removes the "stupid" stain from those used to this feeling. No loss of weight is enough for the anorexic who feels fat shame.

The word "familiar" has its root in family, and familiar experiences make us feel secure. We remain fond of the foods that nurtured us and the sports we grew up with. New foods (such as the roasted tarantula spiders eaten in Thailand) can seem repulsive, and sports (such as cricket to my American husband) can seem like no fun at all. I love cricket and real English tea, kidneys, liver, and blood pudding; my husband loves baseball, hot dogs, pizza, and English muffins, which are American, not English. Familiarity is why we settle into routines, stick with the same old ways of thinking about ourselves and other people, and return to emotional feelings we have had time and again.

Familiarity is a powerful motivator. Whatever the original reasons were for having certain feelings, once they become familiar we are motivated to reexperience them. We will seek them out as if we are starved for them.

Just as we throw off our coats and sigh with relief when we arrive home from a journey, so we return to the home base of our familiar feelings about ourselves and the world when we are challenged. This is why so many people refuse to accept honest praise. They see honest descriptions of real accomplishment as bragging. Many live in a state of anxiety, seeing the world as threatening because they were raised to feel that way. One client told me, "I was trained to be unhappy. My house was Depressionville."

CAN DRUGS GIVE ME CONFIDENCE?

Many of my clients tell me, "I cannot live without antidepressant medication." Is it possible? Where did they get this idea?

We humans are adventurers and discoverers. We seek answers. We want to know why. "Why, Mommy, why?" is the question posed by three-year-olds as they struggle to make sense of the world.

Why across cultures do we seek substances to calm us down and cheer us up? We drink, smoke, chew, sniff, inhale, and ingest all manner of extracts, chemicals, and mind-altering drugs in our quest to feel better—in a word, to feel confident.

The medical profession, faced with the serious question of why so many people feel hopeless and helpless when their lives and circumstances seem acceptable, searched for the answer.

To add to their problem, many patients are hampered by inexplicable anxiety. They see the world as dangerous, when for the majority it is not, and fear unthreatening events and situations. Public speaking is a simple and common example. No one dies as a result of speaking in public.

I watched as a famed actor I knew missed a cue and forgot his lines in a Broadway play. He hid his embarrassment by smiling at the audience, who did not boo or laugh. They cheered him on with applause and open empathy. The critic in the *New York Times* admired his excellence and made no reference to his flubbing on the night I attended. He had expected criticism, and did not realize at the moment of his lapse that he was the only critic present.

Why are so many people stymied by anxiety and depression? Viewing psychological explanations as overly theoretical, woolly, and difficult to research, the medical profession sought a different explanation. It's biological, it's genetic. Find the drugs to affect these problems, just as insulin helps diabetics and antibiotics kill infections, and you have the answer.

To complicate an already complex problem, for a small minority of my clients a biological explanation is clearly accurate. In their family history, there is evidence of schizophrenia, bipolar depressions, addictions, and suicides. They are ever blue with depression or heated up with anxiety. I consider lifelong medications to be a must for this small group.

For the majority, drugs will alleviate symptoms for a time, but their effects will not last. No drug will deliver a life of confidence and the courage that is its close companion. Learning to understand and to act against the habits that undermine your confidence will do so. Add to this prescription the ability to manage feelings calmly and maturely, and immeasurable change will take place. Confidence is then a permanent lifelong state.

For some people, learning to calm and comfort distress and dismal feelings without medication is completely unimaginable. A middle-aged salesman tried to convince me that if drug-free, he would spend his life in bed, miserable and depressed, staring at the ceiling. "I'm too weak. It's too hard," he complained angrily. He, like so many others, was surprised when I did not agree. For I know that confidence is far more potent than medication.

I am not categorically opposed to medication, but I am alarmed by the medical profession's current practice of quickly prescribing antidepressant medication, usually selective serotonin reuptake inhibitors (SSRIs, such as Prozac, Paxil, Zoloft, Serzone, et al.). Medical doctors, including many psychiatrists, think of depression as a medical condition—an illness—that must be treated with medication.

In May 2002, in the city of Philadelphia, an event occurred that rocked the psychiatric community. It also gave me another delicious Eureka! moment. I was right, I was right! (Anyone who nobly claims not to care that they are right is being dishonest with you.) At the annual meeting of the prestigious American Psychiatric Association, GlaxoSmithKline PLC, makers of Paxil (a frequently prescribed SSRI), and the National Institute of Mental Health reported the results of the largest and longest-running study designed to compare the efficacy of medication to that of cognitive therapy. They concluded that cognitive therapy is just as effective as standard drugs in the treatment of depression.

Neuroscientist Helen Mayberg and psychologist Zindel Segal of the University of Toronto recently discovered that drugs and cognitive therapy affect different regions of the brain. Using brain imaging techniques, they found that antidepressants reduce activity in the lower centers, where anxiety and stress originate. Cognitive therapy operates on the higher centers of the brain, and has a longer-lasting therapeutic effect on depression than drugs alone do.

All depression is biochemical. All emotions are biochemical, too. I know from experience that effective cognitive therapy can really help people relieve depression, and it therefore changes the brain's chemistry. I never believed in the nature (inherited genetic problems)-versus-nurture (depression caused by a traumatic or troubled childhood) debate. It's all too much of one thing and none of the other, and impossible to prove in any case.

In my not humble enough opinion, my approach works faster and even better than cognitive therapy, and the results last forever. Confidence is like bike riding—when you know how to ride, the knowledge is permanent. You may fall off from time to time, but when you climb back on, you still know how to ride. Your unconscious has stored the information.

I am not blindly opposed to SSRIs for the severely depressed, but I know that they must be, at a minimum, combined with some form of cognitive or interpersonal therapy to prevent relapse. Clinical judgment is important, but I am very against long-term use of these drugs. For the vast majority, three to six months is enough. I regularly meet with people who have taken them for years. They are emotionally flat, their memory is affected, their sexual libido is greatly reduced and, for many, nonexistent. Some men cannot maintain erections and others cannot ejaculate. Women mostly lose the capacity for orgasms in time, but as they are not turned on, they really don't care. Most would rather turn over and go to sleep than make love, anyway. And do we truly know the effects of taking these drugs for long periods of time? No. They haven't been around long enough.

Once a depressive episode has ended, the person may continue to lack confidence. Medications can relieve symptoms, but they do not alter lifelong patterns of thinking, feeling, and acting. Whatever the familiar psychological patterns were prior to medication, they will continue after medication. Drugs do not deliver a life of confidence.

WHAT'S NEXT

I can help you to calm and regulate your negative feelings, and soon your brain will help you, too. You will learn how to fill out your own prescription for courage, confidence, and calm, and learn to maturely manage the chronic feelings that are the foundations of your lack of confidence.

In order to achieve this, it is necessary to sacrifice. I am asking you to seriously question the beliefs of a lifetime and those thoughts that seem to make total sense, but are in fact empty fictions. Let me give you an example from the lyrics of an old Beatles song, "All you need is love—love is all you need." It sounds so true, so happy, so peaceful—and inexpensive. So many people unquestioningly accept this sentiment.

In the sixties and early seventies, a wellspring of rebellion erupted. *Make love, not war* was the message of young people born after World War II—the baby boomers. They broke all the rules, grew their hair, took off their clothes, burned their bras, cut up their neckties, and heralded an Aquarian flower-bedecked period that invited a whole generation to inhale the love and peace message. Love was seen as a cure—a pacifier that would somehow avoid the age-old battle that breaks out when one group of people tries to enforce its morality onto another group, who for its own genuine and logical reasons refuses to accept it.

If you feel you need love or self-esteem, you're in the right book for the wrong reasons. In this chapter I've tried to persuade you to surrender the old-fashioned notion of self-love or self-esteem that has failed so many in their lifelong quest for confidence, and to replace it with a workable solution to your problem feelings. You have a lot to lose in order to become confident. You have to learn to respect yourself, and not just love yourself. You have agreed not to trust your feelings, and now we must whittle away at the beliefs that cause you to bump up against what you may call your limitations.

Let's be frank: Don't limit yourself by saying, "I can't change. I was born this way."

Let's be clear: You were born to be confident, and you can develop emotional maturity yourself.

THREE

THE FIVE FINGERS OF THE LOSING HAND

Spring in New York arrives with a champagne fizz I never knew in London. In England the slow seasonal shift from the dark skies and damp chill of winter into cold early spring lacks the fast pace and shock jock factor of New York's manic weather swings. Suddenly, on a single night in mid-March, the temperature rises thirty degrees or so, melting the last of the snow in the morning and forcing the forsythia to burst into golden cascades by late afternoon.

Feelings of instant attraction surprised a young couple I knew by suddenly blooming into love and dreams of a future together. They decided to celebrate their two-month anniversary with a romantic spring weekend in New York. As they drove across the Hudson River into the hyperactive city, they were quiet, somber, and withdrawn. Both were lost in thoughts and feelings they believed were about the other.

She, knowing it was to be their first night sleeping together, was excited but fearful. She was feeling unattractive and dreaded his seeing her naked. She wondered if she could undress in the dark. She was scared that he would dump her after the weekend. How could she keep his interest for three long days, she wondered.

He, too, was fearful but excited. Believing that it was only by good fortune that this lovely girl would agree to date him and even seemed to love him, he doubted that his luck would hold for long. He only wanted one thing—not to be anxious. He was worried about pleasing her, for he knew from past experience that fear would soften his erection. Then she would discover what a loser he could be.

People damage their potential for confidence by acting like mind readers and fortune-tellers. They trust their psychic powers, which is a construction of pseudoreality based on a notion of others' assumed thoughts and feelings. Magical predictions about failure confirm the way they are used to feeling about themselves. When men generate so much shame about anticipated failure and supposed subsequent rejection, their sexual arousal quickly fades. They will fail, they think, and could be rejected. Some women rarely achieve orgasm through intercourse for exactly the same reason.

The young couple in the car believed they were genuinely thinking about each other's likely response. The truth is they were only thinking of themselves. They trusted their immature, shame-based, self-critical feelings, and believed their embarrassing predictions would really happen. Their suspicion and mistrust had nothing to do with each other and everything to do with their lack of confidence. This they had in common.

Let's be frank: People who lack confidence are self-centered.

Let's be clear: Every day, all day they sit in a jury box—judging themselves.

People who lack confidence do not understand other people. Seeing others though their own critical lens, they nervously perceive them as judgmental and rejecting. In order to offset their own shame and self-pity, many will pour blame and criticism onto others, and never look at their part in a problem.

A LOSING HAND: STUPID, FAT, OLD, UGLY, LOSER

In a sense, we are never alone. We are involved in a continual conversation in our brain—a back-and-forth dialogue about what we can do, what we should risk, and what we must avoid. Our brain is constantly reminding us about what kind of person we think we are. Feelings play a big part when we paint a picture in our minds of who we are. Smart people can call themselves stupid and talented people can feel like losers.

As his painting progresses, Leon, a successful landscape painter, has a conversation that goes on in his mind. Here's how he described it to me:

"In the beginning, I feel enthusiastic and clear. As I sketch out my vision in my chosen location, it usually feels right, and I am confident about my work, for a while. Later on, I begin to lose faith. I begin to see the painting as boring and mundane. I dread showing it to my gallery, and I severely criticize myself for wasting so much of my time on a meaningless task. Sometimes, I stop work and hide the canvas behind a stack of others in my studio. I feel humiliated just by the sight of it. I get so angry I scream at myself: 'You are just not as creative as other artists! You're just an over-the-hill, boring loser!'

"At some point later on, I will drag out the canvas, and I am usually surprised. 'Not bad,' I think. 'Maybe it has a little merit. I think I'll finish it.' Years later, when I review my past works in my latest exhibition, I'm shocked to find that the paintings I hated most are considered to be among my best. My feelings had colored my view of what I was trying to portray. I wish my brain would stop calling me a stupid loser."

In my years of experience, I have uncovered the five central myths people who lack confidence create and maintain. (Leon had three of them.) To give you a hand and help remember them easily, I laid them out on the fingers of a Losing Hand.

The Losing Hand 1

You have a hand in it. These ideas generate shame and self-pity and damage confidence.

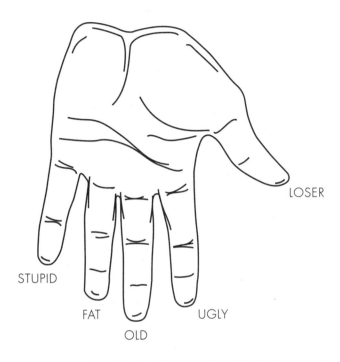

Look at the graphic of the Losing Hand. You will see on the fingers of the left hand the five most common shame- and self-pity–creating, confidence-threatening, fiction-based myths people perpetuate to make their lives difficult and themselves miserable and certain to under-achieve:

- Look at the Stupid Finger on your left hand. It points critically at you. "You make mistakes. You are stupid. You ought to feel ashamed."

- The Fat Finger is forever poking at your fat, real or imagined. Stuck in an overweight mind and/or body you cannot escape from, you feel sorry for yourself and ashamed.
- The Old Finger will tell you only what you cannot do. "It's too late," it warns. "You have missed out. You blew it. You will never fulfill your potential."
- The Ugly Finger reminds you that you are forever handicapped. A victim of other people's perceived criticism, you act and feel like an outsider. Jealous of those you see as more attractive, you are always angry and sorry for yourself.
- The Loser Finger points backward to the past and forward to the future. "Once a loser, always a loser," it proclaims. "Don't trust success. It's just good luck. Bad times are ahead."

Which fingers do you point at yourself? I used to call myself a stupid, fat loser.

But wait, there's more: a second Losing Hand. The first Losing Hand represents thoughts and feelings about yourself. The other Losing Hand contains the actions—and inactions— of a loser.

THE OTHER LOSING HAND: BINGEING, PLEASING, WHINING, PROCRASTINATING, AVOIDING

Remember how Leon hid some of his greatest works, unfinished and rejected, behind his other paintings? He procrastinated. Procrastinating joins Bingeing, Pleasing, Whining, and Avoiding in a club no one wants to belong to, but once a member cannot seem to resign from. These habits generate shame and self-pity, anger and anxiety, all of which drain confidence.

Take a look at the fingers of the second Losing Hand and you will see the most common losing behaviors that result from loser feelings and generate even more shame, anxiety, and self-pity:

The Losing Hand 2

You have a hand in it. These behaviors generate shame and self-pity.

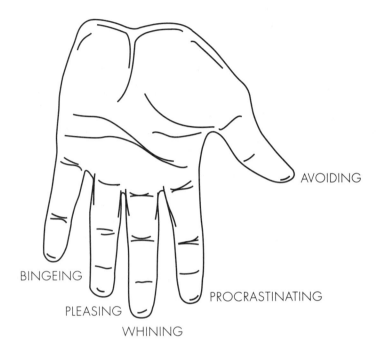

- The Bingeing Finger picks up yet another chocolate, another bowl of ice cream, or just one more french fry too many times.
- The Pleasing Finger tires from doing too much for others and not enough for yourself.
- The Whining Finger complains, resents, and despairs. You feel sorry for yourself because you feel "unfairly treated" and there is "nothing you can do about it."
- The Procrastinating Finger prefers to work on all those trivial tasks—tidying your desk, cleaning the kitchen, staring at the

TV, or sleeping—rather than facing an important responsibility that might not turn out well.

- The Finger of Avoidance somehow refuses to dial the phone to make the call you ought to make or to make other social contacts that might expose you to criticism.

ARE YOU PLAYING WITH A LOSING HAND?

The Losing Hand Quiz

Are you a *self-prescribed* loser? To find out, please respond to the following compliments—honestly. Suppose I said to you:

1. "You are a very smart person."
2. "You look great. I wish I had your body. Did you lose weight?"
3. "What is your secret? You look so young for your age."
4. "You are such an attractive person."
5. "I really admire your success."
6. "I respect the way you respond to criticism. You don't get angry or hurt like I used to."

If you agree with all these comments and thanked me for my insight and honesty, please help others by sharing your secrets for feeling and looking so good and being so successful. Read no further. You are truly confident. You play the game of life with a Winning Hand. Donate this copy of *Complete Confidence* to your less confident friends and ask them to sign the Commitment Contract.

But if, like so many people, you disagreed with me and tried to change my opinion, read on. You responded in much the same way I hear so often from new clients who come to me suffering from a severe shortage of confidence. They may tell me it's not lack of confidence, but something else: anxiety, depression, misfortune, underachievement, addiction, an unhappy relationship, or a combination of the above. I know that, deep down, they lack confidence and are undermining their decisions and solutions to their difficulties. Just listen to some of the self-critical responses I hear when I honestly compliment someone:

1. *"You are a very smart person."*
   - I'm not as smart as a lot of people.
   - Me? No way. I didn't even finish college.
   - Me? I'm book smart but dumb in life.
   - Me, smart? Then why am I always making mistakes and screwing up?
   - Me? I guess I have common sense, but I'm not educated.
   - I'm not smart—I just work hard.
2. *"You look great. I wish I had your figure (or physique). Did you lose weight?"*
   - Are you kidding? I need to lose ____ pounds.
   - It's the outfit—it hides my fat.
   - Just look at my stomach (thighs, butt, legs, chin, etc.)
   - Okay, I might not look fat, but, man, do I feel it.
   - I'm always on a new diet. I'm scared of food—but I think about it all the time.
   - All I have to do is look at food and I gain weight.
3. *"What's your secret? You look so young for your age."*
   - That's because you can't see that I am losing my eyesight, hair, memory—even my sex drive. Everything is drooping and dropping.
   - Look closer. The light is bad in here.
   - You are just being kind. (Internal thoughts: She needs glasses. I don't trust this compliment. What's her agenda?)
4. *"You are such an attractive person."*
   - Thank you. (Internal thoughts: Doesn't she see my awful haircut, wrinkles, blemishes—my failed attempts to look stylish? I don't get it.)

- Coming from an attractive person like you, that's a real compliment. (Internal thought: She doesn't mean it.)
5. *"I really admire your success."*
   - Thank you. (Internal thought: Watch out. I don't trust this one. Trying to get one over on me.)
   - Well, I'm glad you see it that way. I started out with nothing and will probably end up that way.
6. *"I respect the way you respond to your critics. You don't get hurt or angry like I used to."*
   - I don't show my feelings. Inside, I fume and blame myself for days.
   - I just expect criticism. I'm used to it, and I usually deserve it.
   - I hate criticism. I just go quiet. I never know what to say, but I feel hurt and angry.

WHY DO WE LABEL OURSELVES?

When I stand in front of a group of people to talk about confidence, I begin by asking, "Who here calls themselves stupid or fat or old or ugly or a loser? Pick your personal favorite and please own up."

Perceptibly, a subtle shift occurs in the room at the time. "I call myself stupid," the first person bravely volunteers. "Me, too. I'm a stupid loser," another joins in, encouraged by the first. People slowly begin to smile and some soon speak out. The chorus builds, "Oh, isn't it obvious? I'm fat and ugly." More people join in. "Old and ugly—that's me." "I am a bit of a loser, and always have been," claims the leader of the loser choir. By this time laughter rings out everywhere in the room.

"I used to be a stupid loser with a touch of fat," I volunteer, and they laugh at my disclosure. "We all stick so firmly to these critical opinions. What a bunch of self-centered losers we are." By now I am laughing, too. But what are we laughing at? It is not a hostile, mocking laugh at others. We are amused at our own descriptions. We are laughing at ourselves, for in the rational part of our brains we all know that what we are saying is not *really* true. It just *feels* true. It is our feelings that are the problem.

It is clear that some of us may carry more weight than is good for us, and many know that they are not as successful as they would like to be, but to call ourselves fat or loser is too simple and too cruel, and doesn't fit the facts. Yet, people do it all the time. But why do they—why do *we*—do it?

Let me answer this question by saying that how we feel about ourselves is a habit. We are accustomed to our familiar feelings, for we feel secure, and even "at home," with what we know. Our common sense, the rational part of our brain, is always trying to make sense of the world. We have to have feelings about *something*, and we will try to justify the way we feel. And so with insults and self-put-downs, we justify and rationalize our feelings. *We invent something to feel ashamed about so that we can feel shame.*

We manage to feel what we do not fully believe to be true. When the laughter dies down, I press the crowd for their explanations. Here is what they tell me:

- I feel anxious because people will recognize my stupidity.
- I feel uneasy around people because they make me feel inferior.
- I feel angry and sorry for myself because I am fat, and I can't do anything to change that.
- I feel anxious and sorry for myself because I am old. I feel really bad that I didn't achieve more in life and now it's too late to make a difference.
- I feel angry and ashamed because I am unattractive—ugly. And I feel sorry for myself because that's just not fair.
- I'm ashamed because I'm such a loser, and I feel sorry for myself because I can't do anything to change that.

The recognition of the deeper feelings of shame and of its fellow terrorist, self-pity, emerge as I begin to explain to my audience the very nature of emotions. What is the reason that we have them? Here is what I tell people.

Anger and anxiety are fast-acting emotions (as I explained in chapter 2). We get annoyed quickly when insulted or disrespected, even if we don't show it right away or ever. We get anxious and fearful almost instantaneously when threatened, even if we only imagine the threat. Our survival depends on these fast emotional danger signals; they serve as a trigger for us to mount a rapid response to protect ourselves and promote our survival.

Although it may at times be experienced as coming on rapidly, shame is a more chronic, long-acting feeling. For those people who are self-critical, it lies in wait just beneath the surface. Self-critics live in fear of insult and disrespect, and anticipate it at every turn. They often imagine insult when it does not exist, and even create disrespect by unconsciously acting in ways that invite it.

Self-pity is the other chronic, pervasive feeling that haunts those who deem themselves to be weak and less powerful than others. It is the hardest feeling to detect, because we have been taught that it is morally right to feel sorry for the helpless and oppressed, yet we are usually ashamed to view ourselves that way.

Chronic feelings of shame and self-pity are present in everyone who is overly sensitive, thin-skinned, highly emotional, and easily upset. These are the underlying cause of angry outbursts we mistakenly call "being defensive," and for episodes of rage, sulking, and even depression. Shame and self-pity are the answer to the perplexing question as to why people fear and avoid—and often create—frightening scenarios that are highly unpleasant but rare, such as conflict, poverty, and homelessness, and such ordinary actions as driving, flying, and public speaking.

Even our neighbors in the insect and small rodent worlds can be causes for terror and horror. In the past, following my mother's example, I suffered feelings of fright when "victimized" by an encounter with a tiny and totally harmless spider. I would completely forget, during those "visits," that this eight-legged monster was on my cleaning staff, mopping up flies loaded with germs that were potentially more dangerous to me, but didn't scare me at all. It would have made more sense if I feared the flies, but sense has little to do with habitual feelings.

Confidence requires that you learn to shed these immature feelings. They are the barriers to your natural-born confidence. Without them, you will rarely be anxious or fearful, and then only for concrete reasons. You will only be angry in response to genuine ill treatment, and then you will act appropriately and insist on respect. I wrote this book to show you how, but first let me tell you what confidence will and will not do.

Genuine self-confidence, embracing the idea that you are a winner, not a loser, will not deliver unlimited happiness, any more than great wealth will end all your worries. However, self-confidence will bring you fulfillment and serenity, while allowing you to enjoy kinder, more loving relationships. It is a feeling of freedom to live outside of a critical, fearful brain in a world you can fully appreciate.

It will release the wasted energy spent on generating your own debilitating feelings and problems; I hope you will instead use that energy for the common good. For confident people are not self-centered. They care about themselves and they care for others. They can improve the world before they leave it, and they have the energy to do so.

A CLOSER LOOK AT THE LOSING HAND

The way to give up a habit is first to question the beliefs that support it. Each of the fingers of the Losing Hand is a very different route to the same emotional destination. Because they go mostly unquestioned, these emotionally charged ideas lead all of us who hold them to a familiar shameful place. Once there, trapped in this well-known territory, we feel powerless and sorry for ourselves. Let's take an in-depth look at each finger of the Losing Hand.

Stupid

The Stupid Finger is one almost all of my clients use to point critically at themselves. People who grew up with the feeling of somehow not being as smart as others will continue in this self-deception and feel shame as adults. The label "stupid" confirms a notion of inferiority, as if the word itself offers proof. People who lack confidence have a collection of experiences they use as pseudoevidence to convince themselves, and maybe others, that they are stupid.

Many people are shy. They dread the idea of opening their mouths and sounding stupid, because it might confirm a shame-based belief they have about themselves. I have known Ivy League graduates with sterling credentials who claim to feel stupid, and I have met with gifted individuals who have told me that their lack of a college degree somehow confirms their lack of brains. All are shocked when I disagree with them, and they often try to convince me. Listen to what they say:

- "I didn't like to study, so I must be stupid."
- "I don't like small talk because I think it sounds dumb."
- "I make a lot of mistakes because I'm just not smart."
- "I hate making decisions. I'm scared of getting it wrong."

The most incomprehensible evidence people present to me when trying to prove their "stupid" theory is the absolute certainty that their friends and colleagues are so much smarter. "How do you know that?" I ask. "I just do," is the reply, an answer they cannot support with either evidence or sensible reasoning. Some answers are even more strenuous: "Sheenah, I just feel stupid, even though I know it's not true."

Feeling that you are less intelligent than others handicaps you from the start. When you are stuck in your personal lockbox labeled "stupid," you live in a state of shame. You are fearful that your stupidity will be revealed, and therefore you are less likely to participate comfortably in social events or even in conversations, and less likely to make helpful contacts. You dread difficult phone calls, because you can't see the other person and are at a disadvantage without visual cues, and you sometimes avoid them altogether. You are more likely to keep your questions and opinions to yourself—no matter how valuable they are—and avoid people in authority. Cultivating a positive relationship with anyone will be more difficult. As a result, you are much less likely to gain the attention and respect of others. You will be sensitive and often angry, easily hurt and quick to hide from a world that must not uncover your shameful secret: your idea that you are inadequate.

Let's be frank: Those who are self-critical fear and often imagine that others are just as critical of them.

Let's be clear: Yours is the only mind you can read.

Self-critics share a common misconception. They see, hear, and feel criticism everywhere, even if it is not actually happening. Familiar with feeling humiliating shame, they make up stories about how others feel about them in order to fit with their locked-in view of themselves.

The first thing I do when people come to see me is to show them how they maintain their rigid shame-based view of themselves and of other people. A perfect example is Jenny, a young woman in her midthirties who was part of a successful sales team. She had a charming personality, but she avoided going to lunch with her group. She tended to slip away if she saw one of the senior managers walking toward her, fearing she was too stupid to have anything meaningful to say to him or her. Passed over for promotion due to lack of team-building skills, she was silently furious and massively ashamed when she came to see me.

I asked her, "What did you say to your team leader when you heard the news?"

"Nothing," replied Jenny. "I never cause trouble. I just smiled, but I was angry and close to tears. I guess it was stupid of me even to hope for a promotion."

Jenny was an expert at criticizing herself. She imagined that others were just as critical of her. My first task was to show her how her habit of reading other people's minds erroneously justified her shameful feelings. There was much she had to do in order to begin to gain confidence.

For example, she learned that she blamed herself when others were upset. If her boss was in a bad mood she felt it was somehow her fault—she must have done something stupid or wrong. If her boyfriend wanted a night out with the guys she added jealous feelings to her shame collection. "I get so nasty with him. I was dumb to pretend that I'm okay with him going out. I don't feel attractive enough to hold him. I'm scared he'll meet another girl in a bar and dump me." At night her shameful fears would churn in her brain, keeping her awake.

People like Jenny have a familiar habit. They feel inferior to other people. To "prove" it, they become expert shame collectors. Some folks collect stamps, cookie jars, or old fountain pens. My husband, Richard, plays the clarinet and collects old instruments to renovate and preserve. I collect hand-blown crystal simply because I am familiar with it, having grown up in the glass-blowing district of the West Midlands of England, where this ancient craft is passed down through the generations. We collect things that we grew up to be familiar with—including familiar feelings.

Jenny was an expert shame collector. In reality, her boss had always had bad days. In reality, Jenny's boyfriend liked to go to the ball game with his guy friends to watch baseball, not girls. She soon understood and she took her lack of self-respect in both hands and wrung out the shame, especially her "I am stupid" excuse. She was able to reach out to others and share her opinions, and not attribute others' moods to her own doing. As her confidence increased, she lightened up.

As you progress through *Complete Confidence* you, like Jenny, will free yourself from your painful, self-defeating, but all too familiar shame habit, and you will feel freer and live more easily.

Let's be frank: Knowing that you are smart, they are smart, and I am smart is smart thinking.

Let's be clear: Confidence depends on swatting the stupid bug right out of our brains.

Fat

The second finger on the Losing Hand is the "I am too fat" complaint. Every day this idea generates shame and self-pity for millions of people, and they waste millions of dollars each year on ineffective diets and dangerous pills. They have shame about feeling fat and unattractive, especially if they believe self-pityingly that they are trapped forever in a fat body.

Maybe you feel fat, but no one else agrees. You may truly believe your body is the problem, rather than your mind. Or maybe you are truly overweight or perhaps you dislike your less-than-model-perfect parts. The idea that you are fat in all the wrong places is an effective way to overwhelm your confidence, for you will feel like a loser. It is miserable to feel so embarrassed about your body that you just can't face wearing tight jeans or a sexy swimsuit. And it is even worse to wonder if you can ever attract or hold on to a mate, with a body like yours. In bed you will focus on your body, feeling shame rather than the uninhibited joys of sex.

Ironically, because of thoughts and feelings like these, many people spend a good part of their lives waging a losing and unhealthy battle with their weight. We all know that diets don't work for long. People try a diet, don't stick to it, and diet-hop from one supposed mythical, magic cure to another impossible dream diet, losing lots of hope but not much weight. People may stick to a diet for a short while before gorging themselves on chocolates, ice cream, cookies, pastries, and other "forbidden" foods. These binges are followed by angry hopeless periods of guilt, shame, and self-criticism, then followed by empty resolutions to change.

If food is an enemy; if your fridge must be empty; if you skulk to the store and hope the checkout person won't judge you, to load up like a sinner on fatty, sugary goodies to devour in private; if you are too self-conscious to enjoy good sex; if you deny yourself the delight of feeling desirable; if getting dressed up isn't fun; if you simply spend time every day thinking about your weight and berating yourself, you are playing life's game with a Losing Hand. And we must change this.

I have yet to meet overweight clients who did not have the habit of feeling sorry for themselves. Most complain openly, some suffer silently. End your habit of complaining by following this simple rule: no weight references. Never, under any circumstances, comment about your weight, and refuse to talk with other people about their weight problems. Here's how:

If someone says, "You look great. You must have lost weight." Reply, "Thanks, but I don't discuss my weight."

If your husband, wife, lover, or friend asks, "Do you think I am putting on weight?" never answer yes—you will trigger shame, and possibly rage and retribution, if you do. Never say no, either. You will probably be accused of not telling the truth, and it is not your job to act as an emotional scale or a source of comfort to others.

Instead say, "You sound pretty upset about your weight." You can expect something like this in response: "You know, I worry about it. I don't know what to do." Then you can say, "Well, I don't know, either, but I care about you and don't like to see you so unhappy." Then stop—there is nothing more you can add. "Weighty" discussions are not allowed.

The first action many adults take when they feel deprived by life and suffer from familiar feelings of shame and self-pity is to indulge in a binge. Binges are an immature response to these feelings. In chapter 7, "The Winning Hand of Comfort," you will learn how to stop binges by using your brain and not your hand-to-mouth habit to calm your feelings. If you really need to lose weight you will do so with the confidence that you will succeed.

"I've tried everything. I really hope you can help me," said Isabel as she shook my hand at our first meeting. I sat down with her; an overweight middle-aged mom with two teenage daughters. "If only I could have an empty fridge, I could lose weight. It's the only way, but with two teenage kids that's an impossibility. I know I'm trapped. I am so scared my girls will get fat and chunky like me."

SHEENAH: Isabel, "trapped" is just a feeling, not a fact. Feeling deprived and sorry for yourself, you indulge in a binge. This is just a habit, and people give up habits all the time. Tell me, what time of day do you binge?

ISABEL: Late afternoon is my problem time. I come home from work and the kids will have left the usual mess in the kitchen. I'm tired. I have to cook dinner. Oh, and I have to do laundry at the same time. I feel overwhelmed. It's all too much. I am snacking in the fridge before I take off my coat. I have dinner before dinner. Forget diets—they don't work for me. After a couple of days I slip and I'm back to my old routine.

SHEENAH: Isabel, let me explain why diets fail. Unless we deal with the anger and self-pity you call feeling "overwhelmed," and the shame you collect every time you think about your body, you will attempt to seek comfort in a food binge. These miserable feelings are the trigger to bingeing. I can help you with that.

ISABEL: But Sheenah, as much as I like your enthusiasm, and perhaps you've helped other people, I know that I'm a hopeless case. I'll only beat myself up if I fail again. I don't want to go through that again. I will just feel like an even bigger loser.

SHEENAH: Listen to yourself, Isabel. Can you see how you are collecting up shame and self-pity right in front of me? [I leaned over and took her hand.] Let's stop the self-criticism and try for encouragement, not hopelessness, right now.

Let's be frank: Criticism is disrespectful. Disrespect is depriving. Deprivation drives indulgence.

Let's be clear: Criticism is never a motivator. Encouragement always is.

Isabel needed to make some basic emotional changes. After she left, I sat back and thought about her, as I often do, especially with a client who is demoralized. I had noticed that she was wearing baggy clothes to hide the body she hated so much. I knew what she needed to do, and I wanted to help her stop breaking her own heart by letting herself down all the time. Here are the steps Isabel learned to take that helped her to manage the feelings that drove her to binge:

- First, she needed to stop criticizing herself for her binges. This generates shame, which promotes bingeing. It was a challenge for her because she believed that she deserved criticism.
- I encouraged her to stop complaining about her life, her kids, her weight, her everything, because complaining generates self-pity (the feeling of deprivation), which in turn promotes bingeing (an indulgent response).
- I wanted her to learn to say no to others when appropriate, without feeling guilty that she was hurting their feelings. I pointed out that disappointment is normal even in people's everyday lives. I asked her to stop being her teenage kids' unpaid housekeeper, since this made her feel sorry for herself and irritable with them.

- I helped her to understand that her failure to stick to her promises to eat normally led to self-criticism, a confidence drain. Deprived of self-respect, she lacked confidence, and yearned to
indulge in bingeing. I urged her to remind herself that a binge
is inevitably followed by a bout of self-criticism that causes
shame.

- I helped her to get out of her Deprive-Indulge-Deprive-Indulge
Cycle of bingeing (which I discuss in chapter 5).

- Together we practiced the Winning Hand of Comfort (which
will be laid out for you in chapter 7), the program for managing feelings. Isabel needed to learn how to rely on herself first
for respect, understanding, and comfort. She needed to retrain
her brain.

Giving up a bad habit seems impossible at first, but with some persistence it is easier than it feels. This is why so many people are able to
manage their binges. However, I was not surprised to find that after a
few sessions, Isabel walked in upset and feeling hopeless again. "I am
so mad at myself," she said angrily. "I'm so stupid. I promised not to
binge last night, and I have been doing so well, but I fell off the
wagon."

I told her not to despair, but to begin to encourage herself. This included not criticizing herself for her lapse into bingeing. Criticism
draws shame, and feeling powerless drives self-pity. When we slip, a
new response of noncritical comfort can build our emotional muscle.
A scar that sets a wound permanently thickens our skin in that area.
We toughen our resolve and build our confidence when we heal our
failures to follow through on commitment with understanding, calming comfort, and encouragement.

Isabel welcomed the reminder. She took it to heart, and recognized
that there would be slips back into old, familiar ways. A new response
to them could make them into a positive experience, and eventually
her retrained brain would replace indulgence with mature comfort.

I took Isabel's hand. I could feel the renewed hope stirring within her. Isabel was learning to stop generating self-pity and shame and beginning to calm and comfort her feelings. Soon, she would not yearn for fattening, temporary "rewards." She was able to allow her hands to relax calmly in her lap. Soon, they would no longer be her feeding machines. She would lose weight by eating normally, and she did.

Successful people create their success. Almost no one is a victim of an overly slow metabolism, an insatiable appetite, or a true inability to shed weight.

Let's be frank: Almost no one is a victim.

Let's be clear: You must give up the excuses ("I'm helpless around chocolate") that undermine your motivation. Everyone can lose weight, and a normal weight feels better and is a sign of confidence.

Old

"Today is my birthday. I am thirty, forty, fifty, sixty or seventy." No matter how old they are people say the same thing to me, "It's too late. I've wasted my life's opportunities." I do believe that many if not most of us are underachievers. Our negative emotions hamper our ambitions. However, saying one is "too old" is the oldest excuse in the world for not doing enough. It is built on the mistaken notion that only the young are smart, sexy, and hip. Many people criticize themselves for their misspent youth ("If only I could live my life over again"), and they use their age to justify the reasons why they underachieved in the past. They also claim that they are "too old" to achieve anything remarkable in the future. ("It's too late to pursue a new occupation . . . to change an old habit . . . to feel better about myself . . . too late to look and feel sexy.")

These I'm-too-old-and-it's-too-late people feel handicapped, unable to rise from their emotional wheelchairs and too disabled to walk forward into a powerful, more confident future. They shun opportunities, avoid potential relationships, and sex becomes minimal ("At my age, I'm past that") and often ceases to exist in their lives. People who define themselves by the number of birthdays they have celebrated count the years with the Old Finger on the Losing Hand.

Bob, a fifty-eight-year-old man, reluctantly came to see me. Martha, Bob's wife, had called me. "You've got to see my husband. He's acting like an old man. He's given up. I don't know what to do. He's driving me crazy."

Bob was angry. "I didn't want to come here today. You seem like a nice person, but I don't need your help. I have a *real* problem. I have been downsized. After twenty years of loyal service my job is being eliminated. I don't know what to do with myself. I love to work."

Bob had had a successful career as a general contractor working for a large real estate development company. As team leader, he would arrive very early every day to ensure that the electricians, plumbers, scaffold builders, painters, and dry-wall constructors were on schedule.

When I sat down with Bob, I knew I had a hard hat on my hands. For all his obvious competence, this man had never been confident. All his life he would blame himself when things went wrong. He would construct some self-critical, shame-building excuse for any setback. Setbacks in construction happen nearly every day, so Bob was a very tense, anxious man. Now the unexpected loss of a giant contract had forced his firm to downsize and, reluctantly, they let him go.

You surely know other self-critics like Bob, who always blame themselves when things go wrong. Bob is so familiar with his "it's all my fault" self-critical myth that he would not believe you if you attempted to talk him out of his rigid point of view. I tried that and I failed. I told him, "Downsizing happens; it's business, not you. It is a normal reversal that requires a normal response."

"No," he argued. "It's all about me. I'm past it. I'm too old, I'm losing my grip. I should have started my own business. My pals that did are rich today. Who would ever hire a man in his late fifties?" It took some time, but together we came to see that he had always felt left behind and had avoided taking opportunities. He had handicapped himself. In his own depressive way, he had the habit of predicting that nothing could work out for the good. So he stuck with security and didn't take risks.

Depressive fortune-tellers always predict tragic outcomes: poverty, ill health, the loss of relationships, a dark future.

Let's be frank: If you predict a dark future, you will be right.

Let's be clear: If you walk on the dark side, the sun will shine on someone else.

As depressive thinkers get older, their predictions become regrets. "I missed my chance. It's too late." Shame and self-pity rule, motivation ceases.

To complain about being old is simply a way to feel sorry for yourself, and an excuse to stay in your recliner chair, leaning back and not looking forward.

Bob and I faced reality together. He came to see that his view of himself as an unlucky victim was a powerful myth that constantly reinforced his familiar feelings of anxiety based on shame and self-pity. Familiar feeling habits offer an "I know my place, I know who I am" sense of security. They mislead us and make trouble in our relationships. Bob's dark predictions and complaining turned his wife's sympathy into irritation and anger, and he then felt even more misunderstood and victimized.

Bob's father had had the same feelings about himself. He always felt like a helpless pawn in a cruel world. Soon Bob began to face his self-defeating emotional habits. He challenged his thinking. He stopped complaining and started fighting back. He soon stopped disagreeing with me every time I pointed out that he had skills many would want, and stopped blaming his firm for his job loss. I would never accept his self-serving explanations. Bob gave up blaming and cleared his brain so he could think practically, face his immediate problem, and make plans. He decided to join some former colleagues in starting up a renovation business. He stopped driving himself and his wife crazy with his insistence that they must cut back on their lifestyle or else face an empty, impoverished future. His wife would tease him lovingly when he slipped ("Of course it won't work, dear, why bother?"). He always laughed when she did this. His strong, capable, tough hands had taken hold of his life.

You can laugh a lot, too, if you are prepared to reconstruct a better sense of yourself and develop a benign and manageable view of the world. Your habits of turning others into enemies, blaming, and complaining promote shame and self-pity, which demotivate you.

Let's be frank: Never buy a ticket on the Hopeless Express.

Let's be clear: The world is not your enemy, you are.

So, don't feel old; there's no future in it. It is simply an excuse to feel sorry for yourself and not promote your abilities and build a better future. "Old" is only an opinion, but it can become a pervasive attitude. Instead of enjoying the achievement of having come this far and enriching your life and those of others with your wisdom and experience, you waste precious time criticizing yourself and complaining of paradise lost.

It's time to get off the sofa and actually live your life. It is not over until your last moment, and those who focus on death are missing out by worrying about what they cannot change or control.

The "old" can do almost everything the young can do. Maybe not as much or for as long, but energy, sex, creativity, companionship, and fun all taste better with experience. Older women today are sexier than their mothers ever dared to be. Free from the binds of innocent flirtatiousness and contrived surrender, they can attract with power and confidence. It is time to release your inner Mrs. Robinson, but seduce only your husband, boyfriend, or potential partner.

Let's be frank: We are never too old to flirt. So, if you have good legs, go out and get fishnets.

Let's be clear: To feel confident is to feel powerful. Confidence is sexy.

To develop confidence you will at first need to refuse to act on your feelings. Take what may feel to be a risk, in order to change. Encourage yourself. You may *feel* old and tired, and want to do nothing. If you trust these feelings you will age rapidly.

Try doing things you do not want to do. Remember: Giving up is not an option. Adopt a new attitude: Comfort and challenge the whining, self-pitying feelings that say, "I can't, I am too old." You can. Your age is not the problem. Your feelings are the problem.

For several years I was the in-house "get-over-it shrink" on the Fox cable and television network's breakfast shows. One day our guest was the fitness expert Jack LaLanne. In his eighties, he literally cartwheeled around the studio. I was struck by his attitude of never giving up. He told me many old people could throw away their canes and walkers, if they would only exercise today and every day. It is "today" as you read this sentence.

Giving up the "I am too old" excuse means throwing away your psychological walking sticks, calming your fears, and living life. This new winning attitude will turn the losing finger of Old to the wisdom and comfort of experience.

Ugly

Along with Fat and Old, Ugly is a key player on the shame team. Some people tell me that they feel all three. "I'm too old, fat, and unattractive to feel good or do much with the rest of my life," they complain.

Their feelings often have little to do with reality and much to do with habit. The feeling of being unattractive or even downright ugly is usually applied to a specific part of the body. Take hair, for example. Ever had a bad hair day? When hair becomes a target for shame, it is often described as too thin, too thick, or too lifeless. Other hair haters deem their hair as too straight or too curly, and complain that no matter how many salons and colors they try, it never looks right. Many live in dread of the next bad haircut. They dream that magically one day they will find the superstylist whose magic shears will make over their entire lives with just a few inspired snips. It never happens. Hair stylists do not trim and shape feelings.

Men are just as affected by their looks as women. I know men who spend far too much time staring into their bathroom mirrors, reviewing their receding hairlines, skin blotches, prominent noses, or thin lips. Each day and every mirror gives them another opportunity to pick apart their favorite target for shame.

Sexual performance is another all-too-popular way to create shame. As they look down at Mr. Softy, *if* they can see over their gut, they predict a future of failure. Sexual pleasure is a past event. A man may think that all we see is his bald head, fat stomach, and double chin, and that if he isn't an athletic, sexually charged lover all the time, we won't love and respect him. How wrong he is.

People who assume that the first thing we notice is an ugly body part are so consumed with their own shame that their self-absorption numbs them to our real response. When we are so self-conscious, it is almost impossible for us to present ourselves to the world as attractive, confident packages. We are unlikely to attract attention. This puts us at a severe disadvantage, which confirms our "ugly," self-pitying feelings.

To play with a Winning Hand, a serious focus on looks is essential. This takes some time and some money. It means getting dressed properly every day: Cleaning your shoes, ironing that crumpled shirt, getting a great haircut, and replacing those old jeans and stained sweat-pants. This takes effort. It means getting up earlier in the morning to go to work looking great. The great unwashed look, one day's stubble, greasy hair, and a flabby body will only help you to feel the shame of looking ugly and invite criticism and disregard in others.

If you avoid working out because it's boring, stop complaining. Boredom is only for kids.

Give up all excuses. The idea that "it is inside that matters and people should just accept me the way I am" is a losing one. Others make assumptions about you based on first impressions. How you appear influences how you will be accepted. So, scruffy can translate into unattractive, even ugly, lazy, a loser, etc.—a real shame-creating attitude. Start over. Today. Now.

Let's be frank: To help your inner self, take care of your outer self. You are worth it.

Let's be clear: Never, never break a commitment you make to yourself. If you do, you break your own heart.

If people feel ugly, no amount of wealth and accomplishment will give them a true sense of confidence. To play with a Winning Hand you must strive to stop the criticism and to insist that you stop the complaining. Invest in your looks and remember that there are many who will find you attractive, because confidence is very sexy. You can and will turn the Ugly finger into Attractive.

Loser

Finger Five is the saddest of all: People who constantly experience shaming self-criticism—self-described losers—all unconsciously act in ways that ensure their continued failure by undermining their confidence.

I have a library full of loser examples.

- Ambitious folks too shy to offer an opinion or speak in public for fear of sounding dumb
- The guy who did not hear the alarm clock and missed a job interview
- The woman who got married and immediately gained twenty pounds
- Lonely individuals who turn down social invitations because they fear that they have nothing to say
- The woman who waits for years hoping that her lover will leave the wife he is miserable with
- People who stay in losing relationships with troubled partners. Because of their familiar habits of feelings of self-pity and of

being victimized, they stay with partners who treat them with unkindness, disrespect, and even violence.

My list includes everyone who feels the shame of being stupid, fat, old, ugly, or a loser. If you include every procrastinator, avoider, binger, whiner, or pleaser you have ever known, you now realize that almost everyone to some extent is playing the game of life with a Losing Hand. To some extent, almost all of us undermine our confidence with these habits, and we underachieve.

You probably know how that feels. For most of us, shaming self-criticism inhibits our ability to attain or maintain the success we seek in all phases of life. Maybe we can't see ourselves making enough money. Perhaps we can't picture being a good enough mother, father, or lover. We are likely to damage rather than enrich our relationships if we have these beliefs.

Our attitudes cost us at work as well as at home. We are likely to count ourselves out rather than in, and thus never realize our full potential. Lacking confidence, we focus on our own depressed feelings instead of seeking out the opportunities that we could generate for ourselves.

Confidence is the ultimate prize for those who play with a Winning Hand. The goal of this book is to help you to change the emotionally challenged misperceptions that cause your painful feelings, and to replace depression with confidence.

This debilitating affliction leaves millions convinced that their very genes are programmed to prevent them from ever feeling good for long. For the vast majority of depressives, it is far more likely that their feelings, rather than their biology, are influencing their attitudes.

It is impossible to feel confident if you react to the world like a child who turns husband, wife, boss, friend, and neighbor into an authority, a parent whose approval you need and whose abandonment you fear. Certainly, you want to be loved and respected, but it is not necessary to be reassured, comforted, and agreed with all the time, nor is it necessary that everyone like you. Those who barely know you, but choose not to like you, can only have theories about you.

Disagreement, sensitively given without blame, is respectful. When poorly treated, simply state, "I do not feel respected when you treat me this way." And say no more. Do not get into any debate about who is right and who is wrong—*never talk about it.* There is no need for blame, recrimination, or explanation. Extensive discussions or going on at length end up in a blame game—useless and painful fighting about who is right. Expressing simply and clearly that you feel disre-

The Winning Hand 1

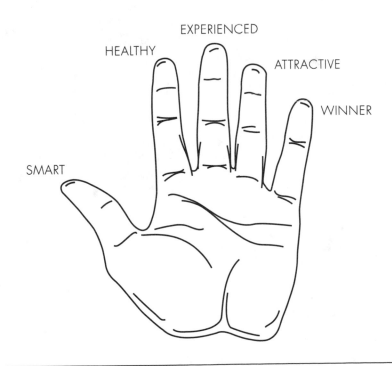

spected is powerful, and invites the other person to listen to what you want or don't want, and to learn more about you. As a result, they will likely know how to be considerate and respectful toward you.

Let's be frank: Difficulty is the mother of confidence. Thank the critic.

Let's be clear: In life, some pain is inevitable. Most suffering is optional.

In life there is some loss, but no losers. Confidence is a natural life force designed to overcome dark times and create what you want to happen. *Complete Confidence* has a well-tested policy to help you overcome your self-defeating habits and to turn the Losing Hand into a Winning Hand.

FOUR

WHY GOOD PEOPLE HAVE BAD FEELINGS

People often tell me that they are making trouble for themselves. "I am my own worst enemy," is a common complaint. What they cannot tell me is why, and they have no idea how to stop. Somehow, or so the myth goes, the balm of self-esteem will soothe their painful feelings. But shameful self-criticism will not be fooled for long with a simple dose of well-meant self-admiration. Like faint praise, this good feeling fades fast.

I don't like the term "self-esteem." For me, it has become an empty catchphrase, hard to define and so overused as to be meaningless. Most people tell me it is self-love, or vaguely refer to it as "feeling good about yourself," a feeling that comes from having been regarded well in the past, especially by one's parents. While praise and encouragement, which are supposed to promote self-esteem, feel good, without confidence they are like getting dessert without eating the healthy stuff first.

Children certainly need praise and encouragement following effort, and they need admiration and love for being who they are in order to feel securely attached within their families. However, mature adults do not *need* much praise, and praise will not change immature emotional habits, but only temporarily cover them over. It is my guess that self-esteem is a losing attempt to apply Band-Aids of self-admiration and praise to wounds that will not heal—wounds caused by a habit of shaming oneself with ongoing self-criticism. And no one has ever proved that self-esteem will bring any or all of the rewards its proponents claim. Like any Band-Aid I have ever applied, it falls off in time.

It took me a long time to understand that lack of confidence, not lack of self-esteem, is the real problem. I needed to discover what causes lack of confidence. My research eventually paid off. I slowly began to understand that lurking beneath a lack of confidence are chronic immature feelings of shame and self-pity. Shame and self-pity wounds bleed confidence away. These wounds will not heal without a different kind of treatment.

Let's be frank: Self-esteem demands that you judge yourself positively.

Let's be clear: Confidence demands that you do not judge yourself at all.

Your habitual immature, negative feelings are the cause of all your problems, and are the infection in your system. You cannot kiss them better, nor can you cure what you do not understand. The questions this chapter will answer are:

- Why do good people have bad feelings?
- Why do they continue to experience these feelings even in good times?
- How can they change and deal themselves a Winning Hand?

I remember the first time I met Chuck, the CEO of a public corporation. In his formal business suit and golfer's tan, he looked like a confident middle-aged news anchor. He came straight to the point. "I'm just an anxious person. It's who I am. No one would believe how nervous I feel inside most of the time. My family is fine and the company is in great shape. Just look at our stock prices and you can see for yourself. I know I have a good life, so why do I wake up every morning feeling irritable and dissatisfied?"

I recalled the scores of clients I have worked with who seemed, on the surface, to have it all. Yet they lived in fear of future failure and tragedy. Consumed with self-critical thoughts, they were forever fearful that others would criticize them and confirm their shameful fears.

Success had only increased their anxiety. With more visible responsibility, they fear that they have more to lose. Their view of themselves clashes with the reality of their lives. Listen to how Chuck thinks. Notice how he creates his own shameful feelings.

CHUCK: I feel like a fraud. I was in the right place at the right time, but just like the stock market, everyone's luck runs out in time.

Was I supposed to accept that Chuck is a con man who got lucky for a while? Must I accept that soon he will be a loser and suffer immense humiliation? Would you accept his story? I didn't. Listen to what I told him.

SHEENAH: Your feelings, Chuck, are your problem, not fate. Your so-called luck is in your own hands. How did you acquire your habit of self-critical thinking?

In later sessions, Chuck told me how he had grown up in an intensely critical family environment. If I had tried to compliment him, and thus raise his "self-esteem," I knew what he would say: "Anyone could do what I did. I'm just a regular guy who got lucky."

Like so many successful people who play life's game with a Losing Hand, nothing Chuck had achieved or could achieve has made him feel better about himself for long. He was successful, but didn't enjoy his success. He looks like a winner—he is a winner. But he thinks, and therefore feels, like a loser. Unfamiliar with praise and pride, he expects critical shame and explains away his achievements in order to reexperience familiar, secure, but unpleasant feelings. He is uncomfortable with admiration, but comfortably "at home" with shame.

Chuck, like so many of us, lacked confidence. He was so familiar with his feelings of fear and self-critical shame that he did not believe he could change. So many people are addicted to feeling bad about themselves that no amount of reality—money, achievement, or love— can challenge their feelings. They will try to talk others out of any attempts to modify their painful feelings. One client testily accused me of trying to take her depression away from her. She was right. Why did she, like Chuck, stay so attached to miserable feelings? And why did they both maintain this position despite evidence to the contrary? The answer is that the familiar feels secure, even if it is painful. I was challenging their psychological security.

FAMILIARITY BREEDS FAMILIARITY

Both parts of our brain's activities, the conscious and the unconscious, are constantly striving to help us survive. Night and day, every second, all the time, a balancing act is occurring. Hunger drives us to eat. Thirst demands that we hydrate our bodies. Lungs automatically inhale life-giving oxygen. Rhythmically we expel waste materials to maintain a healthy physical balance. Fatigue is another well-understood signal that we are off balance. Our "homeostasis," or internal self-regulation, is off track. So we feel that we need sleep.

Similarly, our brains are working all the time to try to maintain emotional balance, or emotional homeostasis, which is a term I like to use. Familiar ways of feeling give us a sense of security. Familiar feelings send a message, "I know this. This is who I am. This is safe." A child seeks familiar objects and a familiar environment in order to feel this sense of security. This is why I, like so many moms and dads, was awakened in the middle of the night to collect a small homesick son on his first sleepover, and bring him home to the comfort of his familiar bed.

As we grow up in our families, we not only learn how to behave, but also how and what to think and feel. This is the rhythm of our lives. All families have an emotional rhythm, and all children quickly learn the throbbing background beat. In some families it is loud opera or rock and roll: yell when angry, weep and complain when thwarted. In others the opposite is true. Faint Muzak is the rule. Anger is never openly expressed. Complaining is criticized. The emotional song of each of our families stays in our heads. We hear it all the time, a tune we never forget. It comes with lyrics, too. In some families the words go like this: "Stand up for yourself, fight back, no wimps here." In others, "Be nice, never upset others, please and apologize, even if you did nothing wrong."

To change the tune in your head, you must first understand the music and words of the one that is currently playing—your familiar emotional song. Only then can you change the tune and decide to manage your feelings differently. Feelings can lead you to act in self-defeating ways. Depressing, helpless thoughts and shameful and angry feelings will prevent you from thinking and acting in a confident manner.

We get very used to experiencing the few feelings that are most frequently demonstrated or engendered during our childhood and adolescence. These feelings become our normal way to feel. When we don't experience such feelings, we feel uneasy—insecure. And, usually without knowing it, we set about to make our very personal "normal" feelings return, even if they are painful.

FOLLOW THE LEADERS

Some like it loud, some like it soft. Some like it fast, some like it slow. Did you know that your feelings are like a sheet of music? The notes are written on the page. They spell out the melody, harmony, rhythm, and tempo. When a band or orchestra turns printed music into sound, it needs a conductor or leader to keep it from getting out of hand. If it gets too loud or soft, too fast or slow, the conductor is there to bring the sound back to what it is supposed to be. You have a personal conductor, just like those that control a band or orchestra, and it keeps your emotional music within a familiar comfort zone.

Each of us naturally assumes the emotional pitch of his or her family. This is known as the emotional set point, an unwritten rule about how good or bad we should feel most of the time. When we feel too bad, we find ways to lift our moods and bring them closer to the set point. When things go too well, we find ways to bring ourselves down to where the set point says we should be. We have an internal thermostat that takes our emotional temperature and keeps it within a range that is comfortable and feels normal to each of us. We will think and unconsciously act in ways that regulate that familiar emotional temperature zone. If we feel too sad, too mad, or too blue, we will cheer ourselves up just enough to get in the zone.

But we can also feel too good. Then some people will spoil what could be a very good time for them. For example, a financial windfall is an opportunity for us to feel happy and delighted. For other people it produces a very different emotional reaction: I'd better save the money for a rainy day—there are hard times ahead. Such a reaction reduces the good feeling and brings the emotional temperature down into the zone. Feeling either too bad or too good gets regulated to fall within the range of feelings that are familiar to us—the feelings we grew up with and became accustomed to.

Some years ago, I flew to England for my annual visit to see my mother. She was waiting for me at the airport, and I was struck by how well she looked, and by the elegant silk dress she was wearing. I ran to greet her and gave her a hug. "Mom, you look so great. I love your dress." She replied, "What? This old thing? You must be kidding. And you can see I've put on weight." My mother had always felt shame about her appearance. My sincere compliment had challenged her familiar shameful feelings, so she disagreed with me in order to return to her accustomed level of shame.

The formula is simple: familiar feelings = a sense of security. This formula begins to explain why so many people seem to prefer anxiety to calm—why they seem not to seek pleasure and avoid pain. It further explains why they think and act in ways that seem designed to make them feel bad, not good.

Of course, you might be fortunate enough to have mostly good feelings as your familiar emotions. If so, you are well on the way to complete confidence, or perhaps you are already there. In my experience, you are in the minority. The most familiar personal feelings— the ones most people seem to need—are the "bad" ones everyone can name, such as sadness, anxiety, and anger. The less obvious, but in many ways more significant, feelings that lie beneath and drive them are shame and self-pity.

Let's be frank: We are motivated to reexperience familiar feelings— they give a sense of security.

Let's be clear: When familiar feelings are negative, they can damage confidence.

PLAYING WITH A LOSING HAND

I held up the diagram of the first Losing Hand and asked my client Sally to describe herself. Listen to her thoughts. "Well, I call myself stupid a lot," she replied, "and I suppose that means I am a bit of a loser. Oh, and just like so many of my friends, I feel fat. I know I'm not really fat—losing about seven pounds would do it—but I feel obese."

SHEENAH: So, stupid loser with an extra layer of fat is what you think of yourself?

SALLY: Well, at times, yes. I know that I did okay in high school, but I never felt smart. I was never in the cool group, so

I felt like a bit of a loser. I always feel fat. Even when I'm thinner than I am now, I feel fat all the time.

SHEENAH: You keep commenting on your weight. When did this criticism habit begin? Do you remember?

SALLY: From day one, I guess. My mom hid my pictures because I was a fat baby. Even today, I can feel her looking at my body even if she doesn't say anything. She e-mails me diets and weight-loss hints all the time. She means well, but drives me crazy. I think I keep some weight on just to get even. She's a great mom in other ways.

SHEENAH: Sally, I can see that we both understand the origin of your shameful fat feelings, but tell me, where did your stupid idea come from? Do you know?

SALLY: I think it all came from feeling so self-conscious growing up. I felt so fat and ugly that I hid away a lot of the time. I often cut class in high school. I would pretend to be sick so I could stay home, where no one could see me. Of course, I fell behind and got bad grades. I knew I felt stupid and had these bad grades to prove it.

From my perspective, Sally was a smart twenty-seven-year-old. She was tall, with long, dark hair, a pretty face, and honest blue eyes. Looking at her, the term "fat" would never have entered my mind. In fact, earlier, it caught my attention that a young man, a client of one of my colleagues, was eyeing her approvingly in the waiting room. I am sure that Sally never noticed.

I was once again in a very familiar situation. Sitting opposite me was a likeable, attractive young woman who was an expert at undermining her confidence. Sally could find no one except her mother who would agree that she has a weight problem. She had dealt herself two and a half fingers from the Losing Hand: Stupid, Loser, with a large dollop of Fat. These confidence-consuming thoughts continually generate shame, which is no prescription for contentment and success.

When I ask my clients, "Which fingers of the Losing Hand do you point at yourself?" they respond thoughtfully:

- "Hmm—I think I'm a stupid loser, not old yet."
- "Okay. Fat loser—got to be ugly, too, with all that fat."
- "Old and stupid—being old makes you stupid."

Then almost all of them begin to smile, even if every single category seems to fit them. "It's ridiculous, isn't it, to feel this way? I *know* it's not completely true. But I really do *feel* that way."

You can see how the clear-thinking, rational part of the brain is out of sync with the familiar-feeling part. "I know I'm not stupid. I just *feel* it. I have a lot of shame. I know it's not logical, but it *feels* real." So many people do not question this disparity, mostly believing as factual what their feelings tell them. Instead of using the reasoning part of the brain, they rely on feelings to reach conclusions. I call this type of information processing "felt logic." No wonder that their notions of reality are at odds with other people's!

For so many of us shame is a felt logic. Like Sally, I used to feel like a stupid loser, and now as I write this I smile at that old memory.

Remember: Shame comes from self-criticism—an insult to oneself. Those who are self-critical imagine that everyone else is critical of them too, and this further undermines confident action.

Here is a question I now ask you: What are the origins of your shame and self-pity habits? I invite you to become your own personal psychological detective. Before you start, though, you must agree to a rule that all psychological detectives must follow: Uncover evidence, but do not pass judgment. The idea is to understand the origins of your emotional habits, not to blame your family for infusing you with emotions that damage confidence. As a kid, you were as powerless as a paper towel, absorbing whatever emotional stuff your family spilled. If your parent(s) lacked confidence, you will too. But by blaming them for passing along their lack of confidence, you'll turn yourself into a self-pitying victim. Once you agree to the no-blame rule, you can start your investigation.

Let's be frank: Blaming your parents makes you feel like a loser.

Let's be clear: Understanding your parents' influence on your feelings enables you to begin to stop blaming yourself.

PUT YOUR FAMILY ON THE COUCH

Would your parents describe themselves as Stupid, Fat, Old, Ugly, or Losers? Think carefully. As a psychological detective you need not only to hear (or to remember) what they say (or said), but how they behaved as well. Write down your conclusions—get a flip-over note pad if you want to play detective. You have some evidence, but you could check your findings with other witnesses—siblings, aunts, or uncles might assist you with your inquiry.

Let me show you what I mean. Did your parents describe you in one or more of the following shame-inducing ways?

Stupid:

Your brother is the smart one.
Don't be so stupid!
You got a B, what happened to the A?
You got an A? The exam must have been too easy.
You want to go to college? Don't be silly. It's a waste of time. Girls get married.
Girls aren't good at math.
This family is not good at business.
You are too smart for your own good.

Remember Chuck? He told me that his parents never praised his success. They took it for granted, but severely criticized his setbacks.

Think carefully. Can you find any "stupid" descriptions your parents applied to themselves or to you? Or how they felt in general about themselves and others? Or other subtle ways they undermined your intellectual confidence?

Every day I hear descriptions of how my clients' parents felt: the family who felt "inferior" to the neighbors; the father who always complained of being overlooked at work; the mother who demanded frequent phone calls to ensure that her adult children were safe; the mother who, feeling sorry for herself, implied that raising children, entertaining friends, and helping others was a big burden. What can *you* remember about how your parents felt? My mother told me that she was too dumb to help me with my homework.

How about your physical confidence? Do the same investigation for *fat*. Some families try to put kids on a diet when they are very young. Did you hear any statements like these?

Fat:

No dessert for you. You'll get fat.
Boys don't like fat girls.
It's a pity that you inherited my fat stomach.
You keep eating like that and you'll get fat; there's nothing worse.

My mother was never really fat, but she acted as if she were and was always trying to lose weight without succeeding. As a result I was too vigilant about my own weight, and I felt fat even when my friends said I was too thin.

Some families use food as a comfort and as a reward. Food is the remedy for every bad feeling, and the prize for every success.

Don't be upset. Calm down—here's a cookie.

You've been such a good girl. I'll buy you an ice cream.

Some other families don't say anything, but influence by the example they set. They are overweight bingers and encourage their kids to binge, too. Food is always on their minds—and on their tables.

Now let's investigate *old*. Parental attitudes toward aging are very influential. Look for statements similar to these.

Old:

> *Life is tough. You will find out when you get to be my age.*
> *Better find a husband soon, before it's too late.*
> *Go back to college? Change careers at your age?*
> *You can't teach an old dog new tricks.*
> *Don't miss out on life like I did.*

The idea of old is not so much about the calendar as it is about missed opportunities, and being too old to compete successfully.

Now let's look *ugly* in the face. Physical confidence is based on your family's attitude about how you look. In your detective role, search for statements that may have implied that you were less than attractive. And remember to research your parents' attitude as to how they felt about their looks.

Ugly:

> *You may not be pretty, but you have a cute personality.*
> *You have thin hair (small eyes, are too tall, are too small).*
> *It's a pity that the women in our family have such flat chests.*
> *You're short like my side of the family.*

The shame about feeling unattractive is pervasive. No evidence to the contrary makes much difference. Even when families try to reassure kids about their appearance, they may inadvertently confirm their fears: "Don't worry. You'll grow out of it. It's only baby fat." Or "You're a late bloomer."

There are many clichés families that lack confidence repeat to induce anxiety and self-pity in their children. Think about yours as you read these.

Loser:

> *Don't be so ambitious; pride comes before a fall.*
> *Money is the root of all evil.*
> *Save everything for a rainy day.*
> *Get a secure job and make sure you keep it.*
> *You will never make anything of yourself.*

Some families predict only dark times in the future and discourage kids from being ambitious and entrepreneurial.

All of these statements promoted shame and self-pity in so many of my clients. Treat them as guidelines to get you thinking. Write down anything and everything you can remember that is relevant.

Let's go back to Sally. Here's what she came up with: "My mother always regretted that she didn't go to college. She called my father the smart one. She also told me that boys don't like smart girls, so I kept quiet in school even when I knew the answer. My dad was jealous of his brother, who had made a lot of money, so I suspect he felt like a loser. Our family felt destined to be the poor relations."

I asked, "Is there more?"

Sally replied, "Mom told me I was too tall—I'm tall like my dad—so I avoided going to clubs and parties, as short guys might not ask me to dance. She was always going on about my weight and putting me on diets. Dad was always worrying about the money he would need to send me to college. I felt guilty about wanting to go. And he never said that to my brothers. I felt dumber and less deserving than my brothers, to whom Dad paid more attention."

Sally had uncovered the roots of the shame and self-pity habits that undermined her confidence. Do some background investigation of your own. Here is a very helpful guide to understanding how you learned to experience your familiar feelings as a result of your parents' style of parenting. Take a look at the Parenting Style Chart and find the style that best describes your parents and you.

PARENTING STYLE CHART

Parenting Style	Child's Feelings	Child's Responses	Style as Adult	Familiar Feelings as Adult
Yelling and abuse	Intimidation, resentment	Obey due to fear	Passive, dependent, unassertive, passive-aggressive	Anxiety, shame, prone to self-pity and depression, sulky when angry
Whining, complaining	Pity for parents	Obey due to guilt	Whiny, complaining, people-pleasing when angry, prone to bingeing and addiction	Anxiety, self-pity, shame, complains and guilt-trips and seeks sympathy. Prone to depression.
Defer to the child	Entitled	Nothing to obey, child has the power	Selfish, unempathic, prone to addiction	Rageful, irritable, self-pitying. Seeks sympathy and blames others when deprived.
Kind but domineering	Incompetent	Obey without question	Dependent, fearful, immature, prone to underachievement, unenthusiastic	Anxiety, shame, prone to depression, passive-aggressive
Respectful, encouraging	Secure	Cooperative	Autonomous, loyal to family, handles confrontations honestly, calmly, and respectfully	Confident, only anxious for short periods in response to a real threat. Expresses anger calmly and without blame. Depression-free, addiction-free.

Sally put her parents in the Whining and Complaining category, and saw her own persistent anxiety and shame as a result of their parenting style. She feared criticism, which she took as confirmation of the shame she felt about herself. She tried to avoid shame by pleasing her friends and especially her boyfriends. Always putting others first, she felt sorry for herself, fumed inwardly, and binged on ice cream and snacks in a losing attempt to comfort her miserable familiar feelings.

Chuck placed his parents in the Kind but Domineering category, with the accent on domineering. He lived in fear of being "in trouble." He emotionally victimized himself with his anxious habit of predicting future troubles, the vast majority of which never occurred.

HOW FEELINGS CAN UNDERMINE CONFIDENCE

Chuck's life of constant worry was a problem few would believe if they met him. He suffered *internally*.

In contrast, many others are noticeably self-defeating and openly complain of misfortune and ill treatment. Some are extremely negative, discouraging themselves and others from confidently attempting to reach out for opportunities. They love to give advice: "It will never work," they say, no matter what "it" is.

Others are foolishly, pathologically optimistic, and make emotional decisions and act in impulsive ways. Many adolescents, whose ability to rationally process risk factors is limited, are high risk takers, and a few will suffer and, sadly, die. Many of us know people who have wasted money they could have saved or invested, and others who impulsively acquire expensive items like cars and boats that they cannot afford to maintain. When they suffer financial reversals and regrets, self-pity results.

The pernicious habit of self-pity is usually overlooked by mental health professionals and most other people in a culture that defines almost everyone as a victim. I faced a tough challenge and I felt a little stuck—what writers call "writer's block"—when thinking about how I would explain the familiar habit of feeling sorry for yourself. Let me try to illustrate my point powerfully and with total clarity. A brief account of a grand master of self-pity will serve. His blithe self-victimization is obvious to us, but unrecognized by him.

THE STORY OF JEFF THE LOSER

A few years ago, Richard and I landed at an airport on a tiny Caribbean island very few people have heard of. We had reserved a car and expected to find it waiting for us, but could find neither car nor rental agent. We managed to hitch a ride with a friendly local, who loaded us into the back of his pickup truck and took us to our bed-and-breakfast.

Our cabin was simple and more or less clean; its once turquoise bedspread had washed out to a granny gray. It matched the weather and our mood. Some minutes later, Jeff, the guy who rented Jeeps, called. He apologized for not meeting us, and promised to come right over.

Jeff turned out to be an ex-pat American and the kind of guy who tells you his life story up front, leaving no breaks for you to share anything, and showing no interest if you try. He began by saying how he had made a fortune flying expensive ice cream to fancy resorts all over the Caribbean and Central America. Enough money, he said, to pay cash for a powerful twin-engine airplane and a fast powerboat. He had stored his excess cash—thousands of dollars—in zippered bank envelopes stuffed into the walls of his Caribbean cottage on a headland near the beach, because he didn't trust banks. "I lost it all," he said matter-of-factly and with a faint smile.

A hurricane shattered the plane and sank the boat, which he had never gotten around to insuring; neither could it be salvaged. It took an earthmover a day to cut a path through broken trees and twisted vines to his house, now a ruin with no roof—and no sign of the cash. He snorkeled and scuba-dived around the bay for a week, but found only three sodden bank envelopes, all empty.

He then moved to another island with his girlfriend, and they started a little business selling her crafts to tourists, but neglected to get a license. They made money for a time, until the authorities shut them down and confiscated their goods in lieu of a fine. He fled to yet another island, without the girlfriend, who was by then an "ex" (I could easily understand why). He took a low-paying job as a water sports director at a small resort, without making inquiries. He relished the thought of getting paid large tips from groups of grateful tourists who had had a good time, only to discover that this all-inclusive resort allowed no tipping.

Somehow he now owned a two-car rental business on this obscure island with few passable roads and few visitors. He showed us a Jeep and again apologized for not showing up at the airport. He could not risk leaving cars there, as they could be stolen. From an island? I wondered if he thought some enemy helicopter might just decide to drop out of nowhere and spirit them away.

He then gave us a very long list of instructions about what we must not do: no parking by the beach—salt and sand will damage the paint; do not go onto side roads—potholes will ruin the tires; be careful when a car approaches on a narrow road—prickly bushes at the side of the road can scratch the finish. I will spare you the rest. Finally, he pleaded with us, "Be careful, my entire life savings are tied up in this venture." We assured him that we would likely have an anxiety attack simply sitting in his car.

When we checked out his stories in the town, all were verified. "You met 'Jeff the Loser.' He won't be around long," a bartender told us. "With his approach to business, no one will rent from him twice." Jeff was clearly the source of his own pratfalls and he didn't have a clue, attributing his fate to hard luck. Jeff was a seeker of misfortune, a consummate self-pitier who had no idea that he has the power to change this habit.

How does Jeff generate so much self-pity in one lifetime? Well, he is impulsive and pathologically optimistic. He does not think things through and never suspects that his antics will get him into trouble, despite repeated experiences. Jeff puddle-jumps from self-created disaster to disaster. When he crashes, he suffers and complains, and tries to suck sympathy from everyone he knows or meets. In fact, what he receives and unknowingly generates is what he most fears: shameful criticism, either openly expressed or privately thought, and the title "Jeff the Loser."

I can only speculate that foolhardy optimism, based on emotional rather than rational decisions, and recurring bouts of self-pity and anger at his bad luck were his experiences growing up. Jeff has a gambler's hope and refusal to ever accept that no matter how much you bet, the house always wins in the end, and you lose. This is a prescription for lifelong self-pity and humiliation, an emotional habit that mistakes false hope as confidence when the opposite is the case.

THINKING HABITS OF A LOSER: COMPARING, CRITIQUING, CRITICIZING, CALAMITIZING, CRIPPLING

Comparing: It is an impossible task to compare one person to another, except for a specific detail or an obvious skill. Whose hair is curlier, or who caught the most fish is the kind of question that can be answered with certainty. Simple stuff can be rated; something as complex as a person cannot.

Many people with shame and self-pity habits use comparisons as attempts to prove that they are inferior, and therefore shameful, or superior to another person. They express superiority in simplistic, subjective, and self-serving ways: "I'm thinner than she, and therefore better." "I know my idea is the right one: he's stupid." "I don't want to mix with those low-class people." The need to declare oneself better than another is to seek a shot glass of false approval, and like alcohol, it provides only false courage. The effect is temporary and never fixes a deep-seated shame habit, but only wards it off at the expense of the one who is put down.

To make matters worse, this unattractive habit invites disapproval. For cynical snobs tend to be unpopular and are often targets for counterattack and humiliation. Confidence is not an isolated activity. Connection to others and popularity are the experiences of confident people. They see others as equals in general, and generously attempt to empathize rather than criticize. A belief in one's superiority is the policy of a guaranteed loser.

Critiquing is the very self-centered habit of constantly checking how one is doing or feeling at any given moment. The relationship with oneself is in a constant state of immature self-judgmental review. We may justify this habit as a necessary process that will help us act to avoid the shame of being criticized, overlooked, and rejected. In fact, this habit invites the very criticism and avoidance and rejection we fear. To be so self-centered and into one's own thoughts distances us from the concerns of others. People who are distant are often mistaken as arrogant. This how-am-I-doing view encourages insecure indecisiveness and a pattern of passive pleasing, as critiquers (self-critics) prefer being liked to being honest. Other people will sense the untrustworthiness and weakness that are the inevitable result of these loser policies.

Criticizing: An anticriticism, antiblame stance is a central tenet in the Winning Hand system. To criticize and blame oneself simply creates the shame that impedes confidence. To criticize and blame others is a futile attempt to avoid responsibility and invites hostility, not collaboration.

Calamitizing: As much as I dislike psychobabble and messing around with the English language, the ugly word "calamitizing" describes like no other the thinking of the alarmist. Normal reversals, such as feeling ill, are perceived as having dangerous, even lifethreatening potential. A head cold must be pneumonia. A planned party or holiday dinner is seen as a heavy burden—a cause for pity and resentment, not joy. A simple invitation to meet with the boss is a certain sign of harsh criticism and probable firing. To overreact histrionically is self-defeating and time consuming. Worry is fatiguing. The demand that a party must be a picture of perfection in order to placate the imagined criticism of others means that what could be achieved in three hours takes three days, and must be a rare event. People get annoyed with calamitizers and often ignore them. Their warning of impending tornadoes every time a few clouds gather and the dramas they create are irritating and damaging.

Calamitizers turn mere insects and rodents into serious threats to survival. A cockroach becomes Godzilla; a little mouse is a menacing mammoth. Even the mildest criticism is met with rage and excuses, because it is seen as an all-out assault rather than as a statement of preference or difference of opinion.

Damaging our relationships with ourselves and with others makes us losers. The world is not a dangerous place simply because our alarm system goes off at the slightest vibration. The fearful can never be confident.

Crippling: In my mind, thinking in ways that cripple hope, energy, and action is the most enduring way to handicap the confidence we need to spark enterprise and achievement. Many, many people weight their wings with helpless thoughts and negative predictions:

- It won't work.
- You can't expect that of me.
- I can't. I just can't.

These thoughts stall their potential and prevent them from pursuing their hopes and dreams. They never get off the ground. If a client says "can't" to me, I'll change their words to "I won't." I rephrase to point out the presence of passive victimization versus active choice. For example, a twenty-eight-year-old young woman who was still a virgin told me, "I can't have sex. I'm too shy and embarrassed." Note the passive hopelessness in the tone of her prediction. I rephrased her self-pitying statement in more responsible words, "I won't have sex. I will continue to be shy and embarrassed." When faced with her crip-pling thinking, she began to think of how she might possibly make a different decision.

Let me confess. Once or twice of late I have wallowed in self-pity and whined, "I can't finish writing this book. I have a full-time practice and family obligations. I'm tired." Add "poor me" to the end of my complaints and you can see how my old familiar habit of self-pity was reinvented by my thinking. I was crippling myself with my feelings by immaturely claiming that the task ahead of me was overwhelming, if not impossible. When I rephrased my words they became, "I won't finish this book." I then felt irritated and immediately banished the crippling thought. "Oh yes, I will," I said and, as you know, I did.

We are rhythmic creatures. Emotional rhythms and well-known lyrics create our melodies. Do your lyrics—your way of thinking—involve *comparing, critiquing, criticizing, calamatizing,* or *crippling* words and sentiments?

This hand illustrates five typical categories of thinking that pro-mote shame and self-pity. All are immature. They are typically found in junior high school students whose transitional insecurity and lack of experience lead them to question, critique, and compare themselves to others in a growing search for a sense of who they are.

Write down thoughts you have that in some way match the cate-gories of the five fingers. Then rewrite them, rework them, and re-phrase them. If you write them down or type them onto your computer screen every time you feel angry, anxious, sorry for yourself, guilty, or ashamed, you will soon recognize one or more of the five thinking habits that consume your confidence. This is your challenge. Discover your thinking habits—and listen to how you talk with others—and then reedit your words for yourself. Thinking—your in-terpretations and evaluations of things and events—drives feeling, just as feeling drives thinking.

Immature Thinking Habits That Generate Shame and Self-pity

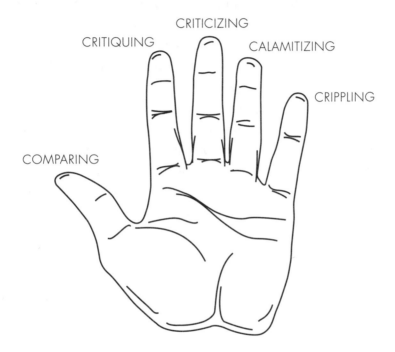

COMPARING: Creating shame by unfavorable comparison to others. Inferiority: "They are smarter, better, thinner, etc." Creating self-pity by comparisons that make you a victim: "I am weaker. I can't compete."

CRITIQUING: Seeking perfection in an attempt to avoid shame (criticism of self). The inevitable failure to be perfect actually creates shame.

CRITICIZING: Immature blaming of self creates shame. Immature blaming of others creates self-pity.

CALAMITIZING: Dramatically overreacting emotionally to normal reversals and the use of exaggerated, dramatic language create self-pity.

CRIPPLING: Believing that what is expected of you and your responsibilities is overwhelming and impossible to fulfill, and expressing helplessness by saying "I can't" generates self-pity.

SILENCE THE CRITIC

Adults never need to be critical of themselves or others. Okay, this excludes a tiny, tiny number of evil people—serial killers, terrorists, pedophiles, etc.—whom we judge with reason. Clearly, rape, mass destruction, and such cannot be tolerated in civilized society, and the law is designed to deal with felons. So, go ahead—pass judgment on the guilty, but be sure to save your old habit of criticism for them, and then you will have none of it left in current life, not for you or for those around you.

"But Sheenah, it's normal to criticize when you make a mistake. Why do I need to give it up?"

Here's why. It merely creates shame and blinds you to the real questions you need to ask: What went wrong? Can I correct it? What can I learn for my future? Doesn't this sound wiser and more encouraging than "you stupid idiot—you screwed up again"?

Let's be frank: Criticism is a habit that creates shame, not motivation.

Let's be clear: While children need a healthy degree of criticism in the form of guidance to learn a few rules, you already know the rules—so keep them and stop criticizing yourself now!

If humiliation built confidence, I would criticize my clients constantly and watch them grow more confident. Instead, I have them all work against that familiar habit. I am not interested in condemning their mistakes or the mistakes of their parents. I don't even like the term "mistake." Errors are simply opportunities to make improvements, a way to learn to do better. This is exactly how I came to write *Complete Confidence.*

So I ask you to stop. Desist. Do not do it. Now I will show you how.

Giving up self-criticism is very difficult at first. It is a habit, after all. So here's what to do when you slip up. When you believe you have made a "mistake," ask yourself:

1. What feeling is my criticism creating? The answer is always the same old familiar shame—your habit.
2. Instead of shame, let me look closer at what went wrong. What can I learn? What can I change?

THE BLAME GAME

While we re-create familiar feelings of shame by criticizing ourselves, many people avoid shame, or believe they do, by blaming others.

When my brother and I were seven and eight, we were close companions and bitter rivals, changing roles many times a day. On Tuesdays in the summer, the soda man would come to my grandmother's cottage in Devon, and we were allowed to choose which flavors we liked and would take with us on daytrips to the beach. We would set up a bar on wooden crates in the cottage garden, keeping our bottles cool in a big, white enamel pot we had filled with water from the rain-barrel. As my father was fond of going to the pub, and the law at that time did not allow kids into bars, we were fascinated by glimpses of bar life: smoke, shiny brass beer pulls, and lots of chatting and laughing people.

We took turns being barmen at the children's pub in the yard. I vividly remember accidentally spilling an entire liter of ice cream soda, as my small hands could not hold the weight. I was attempting to pour the soda slowly to the exact level on the ruler my brother held inside the mug, so that each of us would get every drop that was ours.

He was furious and knocked me over, trying to grab the bottle before it completely emptied. I was ashamed and angry, but with immature cunning I smelled an opportunity. "He pushed me," I yelled as I ran crying to our mom. "He made me spill the soda." My shame died, and pleasure filled every synapse, nerve, pore, and vein of my body as she gave me the sole, exclusive ice cream soda bottle left in our collection. "I win," I whispered to my indignant, infuriated, victimized brother.

This is how all kids behave, and all siblings are rivals at times. Children find shame painful, and rid themselves of it by blaming away responsibility. Unable to stand their own self-criticism—the basis of shame—they blame others in ways that make them sound petty and even untrustworthy. Petty, untrustworthy adults hardly inspire our confidence, but they certainly invite our ire.

So, if you receive criticisms or complaints, or if others act in ways that don't suit you, try hard not to blame. A person who overreacts to a critical comment with a burst of self-pity would feel better if they did not angrily blame their critic. "It's not fair—you are always blaming me." Note the childish tone and the absolute nature of the "always." Expect arguing to follow. Similarly, a wife feeling sorry for herself and wishing for company from her husband is unlikely to get it if she whines, "You are *always* watching sports on TV. You never talk to me."

When we blame, we cause trouble and look foolish. Confident people are influential and get more, but not all, of what they want. When adults act like immature children, they compromise their confidence.

THE LOSING HAND CARD GAME

"If you play your cards right you will win," my mother, a keen bridge player, told me. I played my cards the way she taught me, and for many years I lost. I was a loser—an anxious young woman so infused with shame that I was as weak as a used tea bag.

You can lose your hand of bridge if you keep on playing in the same old way. Lives can be similarly wasted. Failing to notice where the queen is and not leading out the trumps makes us losers. Failing to think confidently and act courageously by sticking with the old familiar hand I was dealt made me a loser, too.

We are all dealt cards as we grow up and we are taught how to play the game—of life, that is. Few of us are able to play with confidence.

Let's be clear about the cards you hold in your hand, and let's be frank. You are in control of how you play, and can deal yourself better cards and play them to guarantee that you will feel confident and be a confident winner.

Please play the Losing Hand Card Game. Unlike regular card games, there are five suits: Stupid, Fat, Old, Ugly, and Loser. Play only the cards that describe you.

Lay the cards out in front of you. Start with Stupid.

Chuck played a Stupid card: "I'm book smart, but that doesn't count for much." And he threw down a Loser card, too: "I'll never succeed in anything important."

Sally played all three of the Fat cards and then added a Stupid card to her pile: "If I were smart I would have done better in school."

Listen to other conversations when you can. A bus or train provides good opportunities. Listen for the Old and Loser cards, especially. Catch the self-pity that is expressed in: "My age is beginning to catch up with me." "I am not what I once was." These self-deprecating complaints are the clues to who plays the Old card. How can age possibly "catch up" to anyone?

Why not be better, wiser, and more experienced than I once was? I used to play the Loser card, and now not playing that game is still both a joy and a relief to me.

Look at the cards you are playing with. Are you dealing yourself a lot of shame and self-pity every day? Mired in a fog of shame, it is impossible to think clearly and strategically, as if we are living in a dark cloud or under one. The future has enormous possibilities and a myriad of opportunities we catch glimpses of from time to time—until we bring down our shame cloud again.

LOSING HAND CARD GAME

♠ LOSER

I'll never succeed in anything important.

If life were a train, I'd be the caboose.

Inferior and inadequate are good words to describe me.

I don't have what it takes to get ahead.

I envy friends who are more successful than me.

I fail to measure up in nearly everything I try.

♣ UGLY

I envy others' good looks.

I don't know who would be attracted to me; I don't have any sex appeal.

I find it difficult to spend money on myself.

I hate looking in the mirror.

Only plastic surgery and a complete makeover would make me attractive.

No matter what I do, my hair is never the way I want it to be.

♥ OLD

I dread getting old.

I have wasted so many opportunities.

I have a lot of regrets about my past.

My age is beginning to catch up with me.

I can't compete with those younger than me.

It's too late for me to make any changes.

♦ FAT

I hate one or more of my body parts.

I'm always thinking about my weight.

I'm addicted to sugar and starchy products.

I have a problem with my weight.

I've tried many diets but I can't stick to any of them.

I know I'd look better, but I just can't stick with an exercise regime.

♠ STUPID

If I were smart, I would have done better in school.

I haven't accomplished as much as I had hoped to.

I'm book smart, but that doesn't count for much.

I can't compete with people smarter than me.

I wasn't there the day they passed out the brains.

I wish I had more education.

DOWN THE CONFIDENCE DRAIN—SHAME AND SELF-PITY HABITS

As I mentioned, shame is generated by negative self-critical thinking. Some people call shame "humiliation." (Guilt is generated when we offend or hurt others; we may then create shame by criticizing ourselves for so doing.)

As I also mentioned earlier, self-pity is generated by the power-robbing thought that you are a victim in life, and that other people or bad luck is the reason. Some people call self-pity "depression." They often mean the same thing.

This chapter promised to explain to you why feelings cause your lack of confidence, and exactly which feelings are the problem. At this point you have all your cards on the table. Are you playing the Shame and Self-pity Game? Take another look at your Losing Hand.

I have been going to great lengths to sell you on the notion that you are the agent of your own shame and self-pity. Unlike infomercials on TV, I am going to persuade you *not* to listen to your own slogans, and I'll tell you how to avoid taking out your loser credit card to buy something that will fail to provide calm and confidence. Now you can see the shame and self-pity product and realize how it works. Now you know that you are not yet used to living without it and that you keep a personal level (or emotional set point) in your system because you are so familiar with it.

"Okay," you may say, "that's enough. I get the point." But wait! There's more!

If you buy my explanation and want to try to exterminate shame, be sure not to ignore self-pity, because this is what so many people feel too much shame to admit to.

I always feel tension in me just before I tell my clients that I can see that they have a habit of feeling sorry for themselves. Only on rare occasions will a person seeking my help be prepared to accept this offering. Many of my clients will feel insulted and angrily get defensive. "Me? Sorry for myself? You got that all wrong. I never feel sorry for myself. I'm no victim. When things go wrong, I don't sit around crying my eyes out. I take care of things."

Others will attempt to justify their self-pitying feelings. "No, it's not a habit. I have genuine reasons to feel sorry for myself. You would, too, in my circumstances, and so would everyone else." But when people try to get me to sympathize with their justifications for feeling self-pity I never agree to do so.

Often in my work I meet with self-pitying couples who tell me that they are having trouble with their relationship, for which they blame each other. Given that relationships are based on choices, verbal agreements, or family ties, they are essentially practical arrangements. Arrangements cannot cause trouble; people do. The participants are the problem—*both* of them, 99 percent of the time.

I have rules for families when the partners are locked in silly couple fights about trivial events just to re-create their own self-pity. Almost of all of us have some of these:

- You expect me to do all the work—you are selfish.
- You always make me late—you're inconsiderate.
- You must have moved my keys—I know I left them there.
- I'm putting on weight—you're serving too much food.
- You always want sex when I'm too tired.

These blaming complaints are tedious to write down. I refuse to listen to them in my office. The blamers make themselves sound like passive victims, suffering at the hand of mean, selfish, uncaring partners. To clients who begin to tell me how nagged they feel and how unfair this is, I ask them to stop. I am trying to get them and, in my not so subtle way, you, to stop playing the blame game with a Losing Hand in your relationships. Here are my rules:

1. Stop complaining.
2. Stop blaming each other.
3. Treat each other with respect.
4. Be better models to your children.

Please agree to try to follow these rules. Also please agree to be more affectionate and complimentary even when you do not feel like it, and to follow the rest of Sheenah's prescription for married couples: Rx: sex once a week at a minimum. No excuses. Let's start with quantity. We will concern ourselves with quality later.

When couples stop complaining and whining (both passive, self-pitying habits) and take action to make changes they do *not* feel like making, their relationship improves. It takes practice to improve a relationship. It is difficult at first, but working together on eliminating blame is essential for those with shame and self-pity habits to begin to live life more confidently. If there are kids, they will have a better chance to play with a Winning Hand.

"But Sheenah, I still don't understand self-pity—what's wrong with feeling sorry for yourself sometimes?"

Let's begin again by looking at some statements I hear from people who have a self-pity habit. Check them out and see if any apply to you.

SELF-PITY: THE HABIT OF POWERLESSNESS AND HELPLESSNESS

The language of self-pity:

- "I'm a binger."
- "I feel pressured."
- "I'm suffering from stress."
- "I get bored so easily."
- "I'm so tired all of the time."

- "I have no time for myself."
- "I have a chemical dependence."
- "I'm depressed."
- "There is never enough time."
- "I'm overwhelmed."
- "I can't take it anymore."
- "Other people are lucky."
- "No one is there for me."
- "It's not fair! It's not fair!"
- "Why me? Bad things are always happening to me."
- "Men are jerks."
- "Women are never satisfied."
- "Life sucks and then you die."
- "It's not fair: Others are smarter than me."
- "It's not fair: I'm fat and can't stick to a diet."
- "It's not fair: I'm too old to change. How did this happen?"
- "It's not fair: I'm ugly—just not good-looking enough."
- "It's not fair: I'm a loser. Others can be confident and successful. Not me. I'm too stupid, fat, old, or ugly. I'm a self-described loser. Feel sorry for me—I do."

Thoughts like these promote a sense of powerlessness, and self-pity is a powerless feeling. Confidence is firmly planted in optimism, comfort, reassurance, and encouragement. Self-pitiers do not allow themselves these; they take it away instead.

BACK TO THE BEGINNING

Why do good people have bad feelings? Because they feel secure with a level of familiar humiliating shame and powerless self-pity. These feelings create a "felt reality"—i.e., a subjective version of reality based on sensations and emotions, not verified by many other people's version of reality.

Why do they continue to experience these feelings even in good times? Because they re-create and maintain a level of habitual feeling in the face of evidence to the contrary. Feelings are a habit.

What must you do to change these habits and henceforth play with a Winning Hand? Please learn the Confidence Creed and remember your commitment—agree to follow it.

The Confidence Creed

- I will challenge my feelings of anxiety and depression, and recognize the habits of shame and self-pity on which they are based.
- I will seek out and acknowledge the origins of these familiar habits, and will not blame my parents or my family.
- I will correct the humiliating and powerless thinking that feeds my shame and self-pity. I will never again call myself stupid, fat, old, ugly, or a loser.
- I will commit to never blaming myself or others unless they break the law.
- I will give up the "right" to complain and seek sympathy unless I am in a real-life crisis.
- *I will do what is right, as I know it at any given moment in time, even if I don't feel like it.*

In order to play the game of life with a Winning Hand, you need to understand that your feelings, not your life, are the problem. Do not trust them. They can lead you astray, and sometimes cause life-threatening problems.

My therapy office is not really a crisis center; it is more of a recovery room. When appointments become available, my trusted secretary, Maureen, will triage her waiting list of people who seek my help according to their need. On some days, I sense a red alert in her voice tone. "We must see this person. I will get him or her in somehow," she tells me. After eighteen years of working with me, she has a nose for a real crisis.

At these times I know that someone has behaved in a way that is seriously threatening their daily life. I remember my emergency appointments that spelled tragedy:

- A scared, insecure mother of a newborn who was drinking a lot of wine to calm down every day and every night.
- A salesman, scared to tell his wife that he could not pay their bills, as he had procrastinated and not claimed his business expenses for nearly a year. The company owed him thousands.
- A young woman who became angry at a coworker and went home in the middle of the day, locked herself in her apartment, and sulked. She unplugged the telephone. Two days passed and her frightened parents called the police. When they broke down the door they found her lying on her bed in her tear-stained business suit.
- The road-rage driver whose fury and complaints about incompetent drivers led to his arrest for causing and leaving the scene of a serious accident
- The doctoral student who could not bring himself to write his thesis, which was all that stood between him and the degree he wanted. His student grants were spent. He would sit and stare at his computer, unable to finish a sentence and surrounded by unopened and overdue bills.

Similar dramas are played out in the press and on TV all the time. Fallen celebrities who screw up their lives at the height of their careers are the stuff of gossip columns. I watched with sadness when the owner of a multimillion dollar retail chain fell into disgrace and humiliation at the height of his power and success. When I was a young mother living in Ireland, I enjoyed the low prices and high quality of the children's clothes, housewares, and groceries sold at Dunnes Stores.

We shoppers were saddened when the owner, the son of the respected founder of the chain, was arrested in a paranoid, cocaine-induced state in a luxury hotel in Florida. In his room were all the trappings of debauchery—huge bags of cocaine, blond wigs left behind by girls from escort services, and bottles and bottles of booze.

Today, he has recovered and is again successful. But the question remains, what causes these people to skydive from their lofty place? Why do others simply destroy opportunity by not producing or even showing up when necessary?

In our own way, I believe all of us are self-defeating to some degree. I, your partner in confidence, years ago avoided the struggle I needed to have with my former husband about his unwise, speculative investing. As a result, he lost everything we had, and I indirectly helped him to do it. Today, I believe that not only are most of us self-defeating, but we are underachievers. Our declines may not be as dramatic as that of the heir to Dunnes Stores, but when feelings rule, reason suffers.

First, we need to understand the feelings that cause us to behave in ways that undermine our confidence, even when we know they are causing trouble for us. If you binge, please, whine, procrastinate, and avoid, and really want to stop, read on. Chapter 5, "Breaking the Habits of a Loser," is for you. You have made a commitment to do so. It is a mark of confidence to keep the promises you make to yourself.

The poet (and scientist) Goethe's encouraging couplet makes a fine end to this chapter and an optimistic and energetic beginning to the next:

Whatever you can do or dream you can, begin it.
Boldness has genius, power, and magic in it.

FIVE

BREAKING THE HABITS OF A LOSER

In years past, if there had been a real organization called Victims Anonymous (VA), I would have stood up and introduced myself, "My name is Sheenah, and I'm a whiner."

As with other well-known twelve-step programs, my fellow sufferers and I would have attempted to overcome our addiction by trying to help each other. What was our addiction? Self-pity.

If Victims Anonymous becomes a reality and opens its doors, life as we know it will come to a grinding halt. Office buildings, factories, and shops will empty. Homes and apartments will stand locked and silent. Transportation will stop.

The world will be quiet, save for the noise of immense crowds on the move to VA meetings. There they will testify, "I am a victim of a self-pity habit. I abuse my brain on a daily basis with large doses of complaining and whining, jealousy and anger. I feel powerless over my chosen binge. I overeat, I gamble, or I shop. I spend and spend; then, I feel victimized by my bingeing habit. I also feel victimized if others criticize me, so I try to please them and keep them happy. They don't return the favor. It's not fair, and I feel angry with them and sorry for myself. I am so nice, why can't others be like me?"

Millions will join the pleading chorus: "Help me. I, too, am a victim of binges. I am a self-pity addict. Give me sympathy. I hand over my power to you. I am depressed and can't help myself. I procrastinate because I don't think I can succeed. So I don't try. I feel sorry for myself. The task feels too hard, too boring, and very taxing, and it could turn out badly and then I'd feel humiliated. So I try to avoid shame by procrastinating, and then feel sorry for myself because I have too much to do and so little time for myself. I feel like a loser."

Others join in: "I don't like crowds. I am no good at small talk. I avoid parties, bars, and entertaining. I get uptight, so I stay away and feel like an outsider—poor me. I'm missing out in life."

Do you feel sorry for these whiners and complainers? Do you believe they are powerless over their binges, their avoidance, and their bad habits? Do you think that they have an emotional disease? I hope not.

I, too, used to feel sorry for myself. I was an irritable, anxious, people-pleasing young woman. A bad procrastinator, I cut college classes to go shopping. I had little money, so I put all my charges on plastic. I wept when I finally forced myself to open the bills that sat on my desk and glared at me. "Poor me. It's not fair. Some of my friends have rich parents. My father will be furious with me." I was completely out of touch with the fact that I had a much-coveted university placement that was entirely funded by the British taxpayers. (I publicly thank them now.) At eighteen, that thought would never have occurred to me. I was so self-centered and consumed with self-pity, I suspect I would have wanted the government to give me a clothing allowance, too.

Let's be frank: Life is unfair—that's normal.

Let's be clear: Some pain is inevitable—suffering is usually optional.

THE SELF-PITY BOOM

On a dark, icy February morning, one of my sons slipped and fell on the sidewalk outside his apartment in Manhattan. Realizing that he might have broken his arm, he wrapped it in his scarf and took the subway uptown to the local hospital emergency room for an X ray. He carefully protected his arm from the rush-hour crowd. The journey took about twelve minutes, during which time two riders approached him. They both said the same thing, "Take my card. I'm a lawyer. I see you have had an accident. Did you know that you can sue whoever is responsible? Could be big money. Think about it and call me."

It is not only lawyers, sensing a fast buck, who respond to injury this way. Many people involved in minor accidents have mixed feelings. At first they feel shocked at the event, and then relieved when they realize how much worse it might have been. Feelings of anxiety diminish only to be replaced by anger and self-pity as they come to think of themselves as "victims." They will then blame someone or some institution, and think that just maybe they can get some hard cash for their pain and suffering.

An obese man used to eating at McDonald's complained to the Minority Rights Division of the U.S. Attorney's Office, claiming that the fast-food chain had violated his rights under the federal equal protection laws, because his enormous rear end would not fit into their standard plastic seats. Many of the worst criminals plead that their crimes were not their fault. They were, they say, the victims of some psychiatric disorder or abusive history, as if this background inevitably produces irresponsible and even illegal behavior.

Daytime television talk shows trot out various self-styled victims in an attempt to generate pity and outrage in the audience. I have been the "expert" on many of them, including a show on the topic "Men Who Try to Control Their Women." Three insanely jealous guys patrolled their wives' and girlfriends' lives in desperate attempts to prevent them from being unfaithful. No other man could be trusted. The guys, fearing that they would be humiliated and victimized, entrapped their mates who, as a result, felt misunderstood, victimized, and sorry for themselves. All of them—victims and victimizers—were angry.

Countless people trek to self-help meetings to overcome addictions that are labeled "diseases." While chemical addictions can clearly be helped by spending time with others who have kicked the habit, the self-pity movement has extended the notion of addiction—and victimization—to all of us.

As the daughter of a hard-drinking Scotsman, I could be seen to suffer from the so-called condition called "codependence." Lately, this label has been applied indiscriminately to all children who come from "dysfunctional" families. I can only assume that every one of us is therefore a codependent victim. What on earth is a "functional" family, anyway? Are we all really victims in need of treatment, or of a recovery movement, or of others' sympathy? In raising these questions I risk the accusation of being "in denial," a term that means I am out of touch with my feelings, or that I am psychologically ignorant, or simply dishonest.

I am not singing solo in the choir of complaint against complainers and the "Complaints R Us" culture. In his book *A Nation of Victims,* Charles Sykes gives ample evidence of how the self-pity blight is eating away at American culture. Wendy Kaminer, in her book *I'm Dysfunctional, You're Dysfunctional,* talks about how the outlandish expansion of the self-help recovery movement has rendered America politically passive.

In my opinion, feeling victimized also encourages too much immature self-centeredness and introspection. Navel contemplation does not promote confidence. Spending too much time claiming to be powerless over habits, and comforting a so-called inner child, leaves little time for encouraging the responsible adult to play with a Winning Hand in life.

You can combat feelings of victimization and self-pity by doing what's right as you know it, acting responsibly, capitalizing on your strengths, and relying on your own good head while not trusting all of your feelings. If you do this, you can resign from VA and live the confident life, free from binges and addiction, self-pity and depression, and without the psychiatric diagnostic labels applied to those with self-pity habits.

TO BINGE OR NOT TO BINGE

Three questions will be answered in this section:

- What is a binge?
- Who is a binger?
- Why binge?

A binge occurs when someone consumes or acquires too much of something for his or her physical, personal, or financial well-being. Most people binge on certain occasions, and binges can be fun, a good thing: too much turkey at Thanksgiving; too much champagne at a very special party or celebration; spending too much on a car, or for that one great dress or piece of jewelry for a birthday; buying a Lotto ticket or placing a bet on the horses that could make dreams come true.

Everyone I know is delighted when Charles Dickens's self-pitying miser Mr. Scrooge is practically lobotomized into buying a much too large Christmas turkey for the sweet-natured Cratchit family. Once in a while, on rare occasions, go for it! Too many holiday gifts for the kids—what joy this binge brings to each and everyone. "Too much" sex on vacation—why not?

No one who is confident wants to miss out on delights and opportunities by having a narrow, rigid life, watching every penny and sermonizing about people who spend a lot, take a drink, or smoke a joint in college. A binge sometimes, occasionally, just at the holidays, once in a while is a freedom—a risk, in a sense. A-go-for-it-you-will-enjoy-it-let's-go response to the world opens our horizons and gives us pleasure, stories to tell, and good family times. "It was worth it. Yes. I will work a little longer over time and pay it off." Or, "I enjoyed it, but I will be sure not to make a habit of it." This is the noncritical response to a normal, very occasional binge.

Who Is a Problem Binger?

The problem is not the binge; the problem is the binger. A binger is a person whose habit either becomes a chemical addiction or feels as compelling and compulsory as a chemical addiction. The binger is a psychological addict who is so entrenched in seeking the substance or outlet to calm painful feelings, that much time—and in extreme cases, all day—is spent in pursuit of what is craved. Many people who binge are too ashamed to be seen doing it, and so they binge in private.

I remember Caitlin. All her life she had been overweight. Now at twenty-six, she was heavy. She had no waist, just a soft roll of flesh around her rib cage that made it hard for her to wear a pair of tight jeans. Her chubby arms seemed shorter than they were, and she had jowls that softened her fine features, making them less remarkable. Like so many overweight young women I have met, she was funny, witty, and sharp. Acting as the class clown in high school had helped offset the shame and embarrassment she felt at being unfashionably fat. "I bet you can't guess why I'm here," she questioned me with a cheeky opening line.

SHEENAH: I would rather you tell me.

CAITLIN: Look at me. You can tell, surely.

SHEENAH: Let me tell you right away. If you are referring to your weight, I have a personal rule of living that is now a crusade I would like you to be part of. We must refuse to make remarks about people's weight. I never say, "You look great. You must have lost weight." I never say, "That dress makes you look fat." I never answer the burning question "Do I look like I've put on weight?" Caitlin, we've just met, but would you consider helping me to encourage others to join my no-weight reference campaign? I really want to change the culture.

Let's be frank: When asked, "Do you think I have put on weight?" remember that no one wants terminal candor.

Let's be clear: Don't share your fantasy fat with anyone.

References to weight pepper almost everyone's conversation. The promise of weight loss sells, but diets and diet talk just make people feel more self-conscious and ashamed, reminding them often of repeated failures. Weight is a personal, intimate, and often shame-creating matter for almost everyone in our culture. I believe it is best not talked about. Caitlin liked this idea. After a few moments of contemplation, she began to giggle.

CAITLIN: Hey, call my mom and my sisters right now. I'll give you the numbers. No, better still, let's do an instant message on my PC to my entire Buddy List. Honestly, weight, or losing it, is almost all my friends talk about.

SHEENAH: My campaign can certainly use all the help it can get. I really hope you will promote it after our session. Now I can guess why you are here. You want to talk about your being overweight and how to solve your bingeing problem. It's okay to talk about it in the privacy of my office.

CAITLIN: I feel really proud when I manage to lose weight. My self-esteem gets a real boost, but deep down I just know I will gain it back, and I get so mad at myself.

SHEENAH: Would you consider not seeing weight loss as an achievement? I do not think we should measure our worth in pounds. Then, if you do gain a pound or two, you do not have to be critical and sorry for yourself. You can just calmly take action.

CAITLIN: That's hard for me to imagine. I let myself down so often. Every day I promise myself I won't binge. I can't tell you how long I keep my promise, but two or three days at most sounds about right. Sometimes I break it right away, and then promise myself that I won't binge tomorrow.

SHEENAH: Do you also promise yourself that you will stick to a diet and fail at that, too?

CAITLIN: I'm a diet expert. The vegetable soup, protein shake, Dr. A, B, C, D, E diet, the all-you-can-eat steamed vegetable buffet, the blood type diet. I live in the zone of being thirty pounds overweight, and I hate it. Oh! By the way, I tried starving—you can see how long I stuck to that.

She lifted her T-shirt and stuck her fingers into her flabby midriff. She grimaced in disgust.

SHEENAH: Well, I can see that you are a founding member of the Deprive-Indulge Club. The Club has millions of members.

CAITLIN: Really? What is that? What do you mean?

Why Binge?

As self-defeating as it seems, so many people who feel sorry for themselves about their weight tend to use food to calm and soothe their feelings. Feeling disgusted with their appearance, and deprived by restrictive diets, they comfort themselves by downing more fat-producing calories, for fat tastes good and sugar can be addictive. This is what I call the *Deprive-Indulge-Deprive-Indulge Cycle*.

I want you to remember a hot summer day. The temperature is rising and feels like a blast furnace. Perhaps you were playing sports or working outside and developed a terrific thirst. Remember how that first longed-for glass of ice-cold water is never enough? How many glasses of water did you need to feel satisfied? Many more than you actually needed to rehydrate. You have the same experience when very hungry. "I could eat a horse," you would tell me, and you will sit down and devour two or three times what you need to satisfy your hunger. Fearing a famine, your brain insists that you stock up immediately as preventive medicine for the future: *Deprive-Indulge-Deprive-Indulge-Deprive-Indulge*.

SHEENAH: Diets deprive, and deprivation leads to indulgence. Deprive-Indulge, Deprive-Indulge sets up the pattern of weight loss and weight gain. This cycle needs to be broken if you are going to stop bingeing and maintain a normal weight.

CAITLIN: Okay. I think I can see what you are saying. But my sister is heavy, too. Fat is a problem in my family. It's our genes. We all have slower metabolisms than others, a nutritionist once told me.

SHEENAH: More likely your family's problem is bad eating habits. Did your parents comfort you with food?

CAITLIN: Umm, my mom did. Food is recreation for us. There were not too many rules in our house, and we all love to eat. We are great coffee and cake folks, and we love to eat junk food in front of the TV. Our house was Snack Central. You know that makes it harder for me to resist when I'm around food. But there is another problem. I am a food addict. I am a survivor of a very dysfunctional family. My dad was an alcoholic. My mom threw him out when I was six.

SHEENAH: Look, it's hard to be deprived of a good dad. I can really understand how tough that was for all of you, but maybe your mom did the right thing by throwing him out. It could have been much worse for all of you if he had stayed. Do not label yourself a victim of past history—something you can never change. That is the root of your feeling sorry for yourself.

CAITLIN: But my last therapist told me that I *do* have an eating disorder. I was a little bulimic when I was younger, and I still make myself throw up from time to time.

I explained to Caitlin that trying to fix internal shameful feelings by controlling one's body weight and food intake is self-destructive. It is a failing policy that sets up a daily opportunity for self-criticism if the scale fails to read the desired number of lost pounds or the appetite is indulged with too much of some food deemed "bad." A criticism binge comes next. The self-centered nature of this quest for the perfect weight is clear. I find that anorectics and bulimics praise themselves for the special achievement of self-control through starvation and throwing up, and angrily chastise themselves if they indulge following a period of desired deprivation. They know of no other ways to calm their shameful and self-pitying feeling habits, and do not understand that this pattern creates even more hopeless shame and powerless self-pity. They truly need to learn to calm and comfort themselves. I wanted Caitlin to master the Winning Hand of Comfort. (See chapter 7 to learn more about it.)

SHEENAH: You don't have an emotional disorder—you suffer from disorderly emotions.

CAITLIN: But I'm chemically depressed. I am taking an antidepressant. I've been on it for two years.

When Caitlin told me about her medication I asked her a lot of questions and found that she did not fit the diagnostic criteria for depression. Later, when I called her doctor, he agreed with me, but told me that Caitlin was too scared to give up medication because she believed she might gain weight. He and I agreed to work together to reduce the dose and get her off unnecessary drugs.

I helped Caitlin to understand that feeling sorry for herself is a habit. This is not depression, but it can become depression if action is not taken. Depression can result from feeling hopeless for long periods of time. In the next session I gave her a list. I told her, "On this list I have put everything you have told me that justifies your self-pity habit—the feelings of a victim—a deprived person." Caitlin took the list and read it out loud to me. Ever the humorist, she adopted a tragic tone:

"I am a victim of food.
"I am a victim of a dysfunctional family.
"I am a victim of my metabolism.
"I am a victim of my genes.
"I am a victim of my eating disorder.
"I am a victim of depression."

She added one of her own, "I am a victim of failed diet syndrome. Diets have cost me a fortune. And I am a victim of 'gym failure'— failure to work out because I look too embarrassingly fat in spandex next to all those sylphs in thongs. Oh, and by the way, I don't date and that means no sex. What a loser, don't you think? Can you be a victim of no sex? What am I? A fat loser!"

"Stop," I interjected. "You are treating yourself unkindly. It is time to stop all this criticism. Let's plan to change all your beliefs that promote your self-pity. You are making trouble for yourself. You are not a victim, you just feel like one. You do not have to feel all this immature self-pity. I will help you now to begin to retrain your brain and learn a brand-new habit, an ace that will guarantee confidence. You will learn to manage your feelings maturely."

We pop a breast or bottle into babies' mouths when they are upset. It comforts them. To cram chocolates or cookies into your mouth when you feel sorry for yourself is immature. It makes you a binger. Bingers binge for another reason: the habit of shooting up with snacks becomes an automatic unconscious act, like the mechanical actions of riding a bicycle or driving a car. You do it, and never have to think about how; it's unconscious. Bingers search for binge food in the fridge or cupboard *without* thinking. They unthinkingly and automatically pile cakes, ice cream, and fatty snacks into their shopping carts. Without thought, they let their Losing Hands sneak into the office drawer where the candy resides. A habit is a habit. Deprive-Indulge becomes Indulge-Indulge. Your brain is trained this way. We will change all of that.

The same goes for drinking alcohol, gambling, shopping, and every other kind of binge. Somehow, bingers' cars turn toward the off-track betting shop or the track—they just seem to know the way. A trip to the mall is relished in advance, and "just looking" becomes "just spending." Some turn on the TV in the middle of the night for a quick peep at the shopping channels. A bargain never to be repeated pops up time and again. Others have one-night stands with sexy strangers; it just feels good—a kind of high—and bad at the same time; the guilt and shame arrive at dawn.

Alcohol, cigarettes, and drugs are the world's most dangerous and most expensive tranquilizers. They are momentary obliterators of shame and self-pity. They take chemical hold of the brain, and silence that nagging neighbor in your head, for a while. But all too soon the racket starts up again.

If you are a binger, you *know* you have to quit. You are definitely on a downward path if you don't. Your habit eats your confidence. Right now let's take your binges in hand.

NEW RULES FOR BINGERS

1. *Make a Commitment.* You have made a commitment to read all of *Complete Confidence*. Breaking promises you make to yourself is to

break your own heart, which will bleed with profuse self-pity if you do. Now, at this moment in your life, I ask you for a joint commitment with me against your binge habit. If you commit, I will deliver. I will mark the path for you, but you must go it alone and you must not stop until your binges are history.

2. *Eliminate Passive Language.* On this crusade to kick your habit, I ask you to promise never to use the word *cannot*: "I can't"—this self-pitying, powerless "poor me" phrase guarantees that you will continue to be a binger and a loser, and feel loser shame. We humans rarely fulfill our potential unless we have to. And so it is that quiet, unassuming folk become great heroes and heroines if this is called for. If someone you truly loved were in dire need—such as a life-threatening situation—would you say "Me, help? I can't?" All of us have enormous wells of potential courage that are reserved for great challenges. You have courage. Your attitude, not your tenacity, persistence, or determination, is the problem.

Courage is in your genes. If you had weak-willed, wimpy ancestors they would have starved to death or been chomped up by a hairy, toothy predator. Instead, your kin survived. You have courage, so tap this resource and apply it.

A crusade will involve discouraging setbacks, but you must carry on regardless. If you feel as if you are going through hell, keep going—you are just passing through. *Can't means won't.* Every time you are tempted to say, "I can't do it. I can't not binge," change it to "I won't do it. I won't stop bingeing." Now you are honest. Honesty is the key to being "clean" and binge-free.

I mentioned at the beginning of this section that you are alone on an antibinge crusade. I firmly believe that every human being has the power to kick a habit, yet some, especially those who are chemically dependent, may need assistance. Abusers of street drugs, over-the-counter drugs, prescription drugs or alcohol should immediately call their family doctor or primary care physician, and seek advice. Also, they should find groups, including AA and NA and respected rehabilitation programs, to help them to begin. Then they can join us, for in the long run, they can and will go it alone.

Nothing feels as good as being binge-free. You have agreed to go on the March for Freedom from Self-pity—the true path to confidence. There is one particular moment you must focus on: When the first piece of candy is in your mouth; when the first glass of booze is drained; when the binge has just begun, *stop*. Pause and put your hands in a relaxed position, for now is the exact time to think about the immature feelings that are drawing you to do what you do not wish to continue. Your depriving self-pity must be managed and no longer indulged.

3. *Manage Painful Feelings*. The key next step to becoming binge-free is to learn and rehearse and practice all the steps laid out in chapter 7, "The Winning Hand of Comfort." By so doing, you will take the healthy drug of choice that you have the facility to manufacture. It will calm and eventually eliminate the chronic feelings of deprivation that demand indulgence.

A footnote: If your binge is too much food, you will agree *not* to diet. In working with people who are always in the normal weight range—a few pounds' variation is all they ever experience—I have noted that they are expert at portion management. They normally eat three meals a day, they rarely snack, and they eat what they enjoy. They are neither nut-and-fruit freaks like squirrels nor red meat eaters like lions and tigers. They enjoy it all in reasonable amounts. Their brains are trained to stop when enough is enough. With practice, you can train yours, too.

If I were to dissect your brain, examine it under a microscope, and then put it back together, I could offer you the following reassurance: Your brain is exactly the same as any other adult's. It can think clearly. It is courageous. It is determined. It is brilliant and bent on survival. It can give you what you want. Just encourage it, follow the rules you learned here, and proceed.

Let's be frank: A slip off the wagon is not an opportunity to criticize or feel helpless, but a chance to understand how it occurred.

Let's be clear: We all get thrown off life's carousel at times. So dust yourself off, don't complain, and climb aboard again.

THE PLEASING HABIT

This part of *Complete Confidence* is specifically designed to annoy people who think of themselves as "nice." When I was in composition class at my English high school, I was never allowed to write the word "nice," yet my mother insisted on my being a *nice* girl, who thinks of others before thinking of herself. Everyone tells me how nice Mom was, and in many ways they were right. "Kind and loving" would certainly describe her, but I watched in disgust her failing attempts to be nice to my furious, critical father. She would make him delicious little suppers before she fled the house to do good works. He was never pleased.

Growing up, I knew I was lucky to be the girl in the family. I was raised not to be served, but to be of service. Only much later, when in counselor training for my job, did I come to see that pleasing others is a strategy to avoid potential criticism. We please in attempt to get others to like and admire us so that we can feel good, at least for a while. Using others' goodwill as an antishame device is frankly dishonest.

Anyone who says, "I can't stand conflict" or, my mother's favorite line, "If you can't say anything nice, don't say anything at all," should leave this earth and move to Planet Pleasant where life is wonderful all the time. On this planet you find that everyone is there to give you "moral support." I dislike this term, for I find that pleasers, who give so much "moral support," are in fact very demanding. They expect at least the same in return. They are pursuing a losing policy: "I am so loving and giving, I expect you to give me the same." Here are their demands:

- Do not disagree with me (it's not fair—I do so much for you).
- Do sympathize and comfort me when I am upset (I am needy and cannot comfort myself).
- Always be in a good mood (I am constantly trying to make you happy, and feel ashamed and mad at you if I fail).
- Pay attention to me when I need it (I have earned it, haven't I?).
- Take care of me by doing what I am afraid to do (I take care of you, so it's payback time).

In time, the immature demands of pleasers will inevitably go unmet, and they dissolve into "poor me, it's not fair" self-pity. They also feel a lot of anger and shame at their failure to keep others happy. Pleasers can be pleasant on the surface for long periods of time, but their resentment grows and they may suddenly and seemingly inexplicably explode into rage. This losing policy both damages their self-respect and influences others to lose confidence in them.

To live on Planet Earth you need to stop being agreeable and instead be straightforward and honest, especially when you must thwart and disappoint others. This can be done with kindness and sensitivity. I regularly help people to be honest and sensitive (empathic) at the same time. If you do not know how to do this, in chapter 8, "The Problem with Anger: Bullies and Victims," I will give you some powerful samples of the words to use.

A Workout for People Pleasers

Here are four exercises to get you out of the people-pleasing habit. Practice all of them regularly.

Exercise One. Do what is right for you—*not* what you imagine others want.

It is self-centered to be a pleaser and comply with your predictions of others' preferences and desires. If you do, this you will not get what you want, and you will quietly resent others for not treating you as you do them. The result? Lots of self-pity, of course, plus a yearning to be left alone in your own private space where no one can tell you what to do.

By eliminating guesses about what pleases others, you can pursue what you believe to be right without the worry of displeasing anyone.

Exercise Two. Ask others what their preferences are and find common ground.

Never feel guilty if you get your own way. Never try to impress people by complying with their wishes without questions. This promotes disrespect, as we all sense weakness in others.

Exercise Three. Respectfully disappoint someone everyday.

Do not fabricate excuses or give explanations. Disappointment is a normal, everyday event. People can handle it, and you need the practice.

Exercise Four. Stand your ground when disrespected. Do so without blame.

The confident person shapes relationships maturely. Immature adults, like kids, please others and do an awful lot of things they would rather not. Mature people are honest about what they want and do not want. Their honesty helps others to understand and respect them.

Let's be frank: Always think no before you say yes.

Let's be clear: Offer or accept others' requests and invitations carefully and cautiously. Cancel rarely, if ever.

WHINING

Margo was a pleaser and a self-pitying binger, but it was her habit of complaining that caught my attention when she came to see me. She was a true whiner. Later on, I would tease her about her PMS, not the menstrual kind, but rather Poor Me Syndrome.

When she had finished complaining about her boss, her current boyfriend, Dan, his parents, and her "ungrateful" grown daughter, she would end with a repetitious chorus: "I never have enough time. There's no time for me. I need to get away and do nothing. I can't stand my life. 'They' [this collective noun seemed to include all of her close relationships and people at work] are so demanding I can't do my job, put up with the commute, cook, and clean, pick up after Dan, and mind my grandchild any time my daughter wants a day to herself. She has it easy—I have no time. They just take me for granted."

It is a proven fact that many women carry a huge burden of responsibility. A recent study from the University of Michigan found that women on average did twenty-seven hours of housework each week, while men averaged only seventeen; in addition, women averaged twenty-four hours of paid work outside the home. I needed more facts about Margo's responsibilities in order to better understand her unhappy life. Clearly, Margo felt overwhelmed by all she wanted to accomplish.

But finding more time for herself was a suspect solution to her self-pity complaints, for Margo had complained her way through a vacation she and Dan took last winter. As usual, she didn't like the hotel, or her room. She felt the food was not up to par, and she didn't have enough legroom on the plane. Dan wanted to play golf and veg out. She complained of his lack of energy and inattention to her: "This is the only time I have to relax all year, and I had to spend so much time buying gifts for those back home. They expect it."

I realized that if Margo were Queen Elizabeth II, she would whine about the weight of the crown, the drafty palace, and all those boring events she had to show up for. She would want to abdicate, but would instead continue to reign, and complain, which is what she is familiar with doing.

Self-pitying complainers have a *habit*. Their lives are not the problem, their feelings are. They set themselves up to feel like victims.

I told Margo three things:

- She has just as much time as everyone else on this planet. Although I meant "as much time each day," she continued her complaint and replied, "Oh, no. I'm fifty-three. There is less than half of my life left. There will not be time for me to do what I want to do before I die."

- I pointed out to Margo that she chose to take on too much and by so doing could complain and criticize others. "You don't understand," she responded. "I have no choice. Who else will do it all if I don't?" I knew from experience that it is practically impossible to talk a complainer out of the habit that makes them unhappy, tired out, and frankly hard to listen to. So, when she took a breath, I told her:

- You need to stop complaining, now and forever. She looked at me open-mouthed and wide-eyed, in a true state of minor shock. Then she spoke, "I would have nothing to say—nothing at all."

Margo had never thought about her complaining ways until I pointed them out to her. She came to recognize that complaining is self-pity spoken out loud, and that it can annoy other people. She also realized how annoyed she got at people who did not give her the sympathy she thought she deserved. Using her new self-understanding, and by applying the Winning Hand of Comfort, she stopped complaining and started to get along better with Dan and with others.

Please follow her example, and stop complaining. Recognize your self-pitying ways and learn from *Complete Confidence* that you suffer from a chronic emotional habit and need to thoroughly learn and practice the brain retraining program I lay out for you in chapter 7, "The Winning Hand of Comfort."

PROCRASTINATION

Procrastinators put off doing what they have agreed to do or what they know they should do. Unopened bills lie on their desks, preparing to shock and scare them when opened. Unwritten thank-you cards wait for time that is never available; they never get the attention they deserve. Homes and apartments humiliate their occupants, who always mean to clean up but seldom do. Procrastinators have grass that grows faster, clothes that need mending more often, too many dishes to wash, and checkbooks in constant need of balancing.

Procrastinators sleep too much, read too much, watch TV programs they don't even like, and binge for the comfort that they never find. "It's not fair, it's too much for me. I can't take it." They are all members of OWA—Overwhelmed Anonymous. Self-pity and resentment wash over them in tidal waves. "I will, I will do it tomorrow." They most likely won't.

Procrastinators are troublemakers. Their noncompliance with reasonable expectations annoys others, who will inevitably criticize them. Procrastinators respond either by blaming themselves—and creating guilt and shame—or by angrily blaming their critics, calling them unreasonable, bossy, and unkind. In this way they regenerate their familiar "poor me, I'm hard done by" self-pity.

Which Kind of Procrastinator Are You?

Type I: The Compulsive Type. Compulsive folk are worriers. They dread being criticized by others, so are precise and fussy about the tasks they undertake. They seek a "perfect" product, which must be squeaky clean and criticism-free. They are poor delegators. They do not believe that others can meet their standards. As a result they are always overworked, they never have enough time. Their seeking of perfection in order to avoid admonition and to gain admiration from others makes them super self-critics and chronic self-pitiers.

They will criticize and put the rest of us to shame. To them we are lazy, sloppy, inefficient, stupid, messy, irresponsible, careless, etc. Most often, this disapproval is not expressed directly, for this would ignite our criticism of them. We can only sense their tight-lipped disapproval by their attitude and air of disdain.

Compulsive-type procrastinators will always be responsible and eventually deliver, but their overattention to detail and perfection-seeking ways make them resentful and sorry for themselves. And they may miss deadlines because all that detail and perfection takes too much time, and costs their employers too much money. They often fool themselves with a foolish and surprising myth: "I work better under pressure. I like to pull all-nighters—I produce good stuff that way."

They certainly do not. The overtired and overtaxed brain will falter. Note how your memory can suffer when you are fatigued. It certainly does not appreciate all the caffeine and lack of rejuvenating sleep the brain requires. These procrastinators have a late habit they need to break. They must respect and care for their brains. To calm their fears and gain confidence, they need the Winning Hand of Comfort.

Type II: The Slacker Type. Humans are not naturally lazy. It simply makes no sense that our survival-seeking genes would have laziness programmed into them. In the past, slackers would have starved to death or have been bumped off by the tribe. Laziness *can* be a binge habit, however. So-called slackers want to do only what they want, usually what is fun. This is what children do when left to their own devices. Many slackers had far too much responsibility as children, having to substitute for their own negligent parents. They will avoid responsibilities and chores when they are adults. Others had no responsibilities and were spoiled as children (look at your Parenting Style Chart in chapter 4), and as adults they spoil themselves. This is upsetting to those around them who angrily do more of the work. Their relationships are filled with conflict as a result.

Type III: The Rebellious Type. Like teenagers, rebellious procrastinators are oppositional. Some of them passively rebel against others, especially those who have power and influence, such as bosses, spouses, and friends. They will show up late, miss deadlines, break promises, and explain away any inconvenience they cause with the universal excuse "I forgot." As you read this sentence, a great chorus of self-pitying procrastinators are right now excusing themselves from duty and responsibility. All of their excuses have a familiar ring:

- "I'm sorry. I forgot."
- "I'm only human. What do you expect from me?"
- "You should have reminded me. I have so much to do. I can't be expected to remember everything."
- "Sorry this is late. I had the flu, the baby was sick, my computer crashed, my car wouldn't start, and several dogs prefer my homework to dog food."

If we do not accept these sympathy-seeking explanations, we can expect an explosion of blame, a tantrum, or a silent sulk:

- "You are such a nag."
- "You expect me to do everything."
- "Why are you making such a big deal of it?"
- "Stop complaining. I'll do it tomorrow. Trust me."

Despite these angry defensive reactions, it is better not to believe these excuses. All humans are *brilliant* and have remarkable *memories*. A procrastinator has a "forgetful" habit—a pattern based on deep-seated, self-centered, immature feelings of self-pity and resentment about *having* to do what others want: "I don't have to do what others expect of me. I want to do what *I* want. I want my own space."

I find that procrastinators hate conforming to their own rules, too. Yes, they rebel against themselves. Everyone has a set of personal rules of living—these are ideas, sometimes unspoken, about what should and should not be done. Most people have the opinion (or personal rule) that it is right to be cooperative and to keep promises. Yet, procrastinators find themselves feeling resentful and resist conforming to these rules. They sincerely believe in cooperating and keeping promises, and so their feelings and actions mystify them. "Why don't I do what I know to be right? It's what I really want to do," they ask me. It is clear to both of us that doing what one believes to be right would promote confident actions. Here is what I tell them:

Rebels get a sense of power from acting in noncompliant ways. However, the power is not based on declaring honestly and openly what they want. It is the passive form of power—the power to thwart and frustrate others. Like teenagers, whose actual power in the family is and should be limited, procrastinators can only derive power from disagreement and opposition.

And I do not just mean noncompliance with others' requests, expectations, or demands. Rebellious procrastinators fail to comply with their own view of what is right and responsible. Even conforming to their own rules, goals, and promises makes them feel like powerless losers.

Let's be frank: Rebels feel victimized by some form of authority; they feel annoyed and put upon.

Let's be clear: A rebel's only cause is a false feeling of power.

Boot Camp for the Procrastinating Brain

Avoiders avoid people, but procrastinators avoid responsibility. The very worst decision a procrastinator can make is to set goals. Getting organized is *not* the cure for procrastination. Goals are demands that go unmet and fade into broken promises that result in familiar shameful feelings and a sense of hopelessness. You cannot solve a psychological problem with a logical solution. Humans are not Palm Pilots with legs. Procrastinators will not stick for long to rigid timetables that spell out hour by hour what must be accomplished.

Every year, at the end of December, I receive a call from a friendly journalist or TV producer asking me to advise people on how to keep their New Year's resolutions. My answer is always the same: Don't make resolutions—you'll only feel ashamed when you break them, and almost everyone does.

So, throw away your time-management manuals and let's pull up the emotional root of your procrastination problem. In order to gain confidence, you need to stop trusting your feelings of self-pity and resentment, and think rationally and maturely. This means recognizing that you feel sorry for yourself and annoyed if you perceive a task you face as difficult, time-consuming, boring, and repetitious. Your resentment will cause you to procrastinate. In time, the incomplete task will cause you to have other immature feelings of ongoing, nagging guilt and miserable self-critical shame. These feelings nag continuously and prevent your brilliant brain from creative thinking and positive problem solving. The rest of us who do not procrastinate are ahead of you, and the gap is widening as you play with a Losing Hand.

It is equally immature and a loser policy to believe that your notion of achieving perfection will protect you from criticism. Criticism is unavoidable, so deal with it honestly and ease the shame it may cause by applying an emotional salve of calm, provided by the Winning Hand of Comfort in chapter 7.

Here are the green lights you need to turn on to give you permission to rev up and get going:

1. I will stop avoiding discipline, from you and others, and accept it maturely.
2. I will stop criticizing myself, and practice accepting others' criticism calmly and maturely. Blaming and complaining must end.
3. I will stop trying to make things perfect, and get them finished in a timely fashion.
4. I will stop, stop, stop making excuses to avoid what is central and to avoid wasting time with the peripheral.
5. I will stop making excuses to you or anyone.
6. I will do anything I choose to do—cheerfully.
7. I will be honest and own up if I procrastinate. No lies. No excuses.

To go forward you need to learn these Seven Commitments by heart. Rehearse them and carry them with you at all times.

Let's be frank: Promises are *not* made to be broken.
Let's be clear: Any act of self-control is a mark of self-respect.

AVOIDING

SERENA: My grandmother, who raised me, lived in fear of what the neighbors might think. She gave me so much that I will never blame her, but I know I get my shyness from her.

SHEENAH: I don't blame parents or grandparents, either. We simply absorb their feelings and ways of responding to them. Your grandma sounds fearful of the world, and you tell me that she avoids people if she does not feel secure in their company.

SERENA: I am so like her. My avoidance is getting in my way, as you know. I didn't even go to my high school graduation, and when I graduated from college my grandma couldn't come, as she is too scared to fly. I am, too, but I do it if I have to. She felt so guilty, and we were both sad about it. I had a video made and she plays it over and over. She is so proud of me.

SHEENAH: Knowing you, I can see why she's proud of you, but we do need to have you become less fearful and more confident.

SERENA: That would be great, but it doesn't seem possible.

SHEENAH: Tell me everything that you avoid.

SERENA: Well, here goes. I avoid going out much. I spend time after work on my computer or watching TV. I rush home after work. I avoid dating. I feel so uptight around guys, especially if I find them attractive. I avoid them, or I get sort of sarcastic, even nasty. I avoid speaking up to my boss, even though she is a really kind person and she asks for my opinions. I am so scared of disappointing her by saying something stupid. Oh, and I hate the weekly department meeting. I never say a word. That's not good for my future. My boss told me I need to feel more confident and contribute. And finally, I avoid going out to lunch with the people at work—I take a sandwich with me—I am scared they will think I am boring. I don't have anything interesting to say. They make plans for weekends, and I am not included. Someone told me they think I feel superior and I'm arrogant. I was so upset by that I cried all night. I'm just shy. Sheenah, I'm lonely, and I feel like a loser. I know I'm smart enough, and I could be a good friend and girlfriend, but I am so damn nervous—kind of paranoid. I can't imagine having sex, I'm so uptight. I always expect something embarrassing will happen, so I hide out.

SHEENAH: Do you ask yourself, what exactly are you afraid of in social situations?

SERENA: I think I will be ignored, left out, and just stand there, blushing for everyone to see and criticize, of course. Reject me, I suppose.

SHEENAH: So, like your grandma, you're afraid of your neighbors, too.

Here is how we attacked Serena's avoidance problem. I laid out for Serena the emotions that barred her from being courageous and confident. We began by understanding her ongoing fear. Serena felt very vulnerable around others. She believed that others were as critical of her as she was. She was also scared that she might act in a way that would embarrass herself and anger others. She felt panicky whenever she thought someone was irritated with her. She would never return unwanted purchases to stores in case the salesperson might be mad at her. She always felt that everyone was looking at her cynically and dis-approvingly. Her response to others' occasional complaints or criti-cism was silence or tears. She usually blamed herself when this happened.

She loved to be at home, safe from what she saw as a hostile world. The only thing she feared there was the telephone. Its ring would cause her stomach to get tense. She was scared to answer it, and always kept the answering machine on so that she could screen her calls and avoid anyone who might want her to do anything she was afraid of—such as chat with them, what would she have to say? Or, worse still, make a date. She couldn't say no—that might upset people—so she just avoided them.

A week later, I saw her name on my daily appointment list. As I went out to greet her, I noted an air of dejection. "It's not your fault," she was quick to tell me. "I went to work and I ran home. I did noth-ing on the weekend. I'm such a loser. I feel even worse than I did be-fore I met you. I declare myself a hopeless case. I'm wasting your time and my money." I could see that Serena was mired in guilt and shame.

I also realized that both she and I had underestimated how fright-ening it would be for Serena to relinquish the only defense she had to protect herself from a world she believed was critical and uncaring. She could tell me that, on an intellectual level, she did not believe this about the world, but her feelings were so real to her, so palpable, that she could not ignore them. I sat back and took a deep breath.

SHEENAH: Serena, we cannot give up. We must start over. You are not a loser—you certainly lost this time, but we can and will learn from this setback. There are many setbacks on the road to confidence, and shame is what they cause. So, we can beat that system by simply gleaning information from this experience. Remember, no blame and no loser labels are al-lowed. Back to square one.

SERENA: I tried to turn on those seven green light suggestions of yours—the ones for the procrastinating brain. But I could not get started and move forward.

SHEENAH: Your fear kept you stuck at the stop sign. Let's begin by explaining why it's easier for you to stay in a place that makes you miserable—lonely and scared and envious of others who are out having fun and meeting guys. Your brain, when you were a young girl, was trained to think and feel in a way that protects you. Your well-meaning grandma saw the world as dangerous, at least psychologically. She saw others as judgmental and critical. She must have been pretty critical of herself to fear others' censure so much.

SERENA: She was scared of everything. She never learned to drive, and is terrified that I will have a road accident. I am not as bad as that, but I hate to be a passenger in someone else's car.

SHEENAH: Your brain overreacts. It sends out warning signals: be careful, hide, avoid. As a little girl you were wise to listen. Now your brain is running an unnecessary protection racket, and you must retrain it.

SERENA: That sounds possible and impossible at the same time.

SHEENAH: We have to train you in a new routine. A brain workout program that, if you persist, will work, and will never stop protecting you in a new and mature way. By associating fear (of victimization) with calm and comfort, a new brain algorithm will develop. Fear—calm—fear—calm. It would take time, for your fears are psychological, not logical, and require a psychological response. I think I pushed you forward too soon in our last session, and I apologize for that.

SERENA: I think you were responding to my desperation and frustration.

SHEENAH: Perhaps. But I learned, and you have learned more about your fear habit.

SERENA (telling me that she felt like a butterfly in a glass case, pinned down by her fears): I am trapped and alive, but cannot seem to free myself.

We set no more tasks for her for a while. Serena was pinned down by her feelings. She needed to master all the steps of the Winning Hand of Comfort, which I lay out for you in chapter 7. Retraining one's brain is not easy, but it is essential. Serena made great efforts and learned after much practice to calm down and comfort her automatic fear of humiliation (shame) and victimization (self-pity). The world

The Winning Hand 2

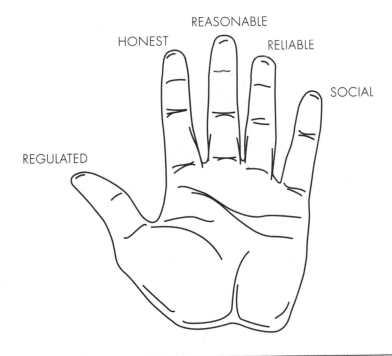

seemed less dangerous to her, and she began to slowly and courageously face each and every one of her fears. She found that the anticipation of doing what she was so anxious about was far worse than the act itself.

Let's review the five habits of a loser—bingeing, pleasing, whining, procrastinating, and avoiding. These self-limiting habits must be replaced with confidence.

You have committed to take the steps outlined in this chapter, all of which will change your life. Let's take a look at what happens when these binges and self-defeating habits are relinquished.

Let's be frank: Blessed are the meek, for they make great scapegoats.

Let's be clear: "All vigorous and ambitious men live by considering that anything is within their capability," Alan Clark, *Diaries*.

SIX

MANAGING YOUR FEELINGS

I want you to get high.

Come on. Just try my uppers and my tranquilizers. They are really special. You can chill out and feel powerful.

Guess what. This stuff makes you feel good. It will take you to a really cool, confident place. Interested? Want to hear more?

My drug will change your brain chemistry, permanently, and you will never feel the same again. Look, I'm a reliable dealer. I'll set you up with all the paraphernalia you need to get started.

But wait—there's more! I will teach you how to make your own supply. Why don't you try it? There's no money involved—just some sweat equity. It could be the ride of your life. Just imagine, you will be able to do everything you are scared of—that's right, everything.

If partying isn't your scene, perhaps you get your emotional fix some other way. It is far more respectable and responsible, let alone legal, to get your drugs from your doctor. You hope that he or she, by writing a few words on a small pad of paper, can provide you with enduring comfort—but can they?

Downers and tranquilizers will certainly calm anxiety. Uppers and antidepressants will lift feelings of hopelessness for about 60 percent of those that take them. Side effects are minimal in the short term. Over time, however, almost everyone will experience considerable side effects. For example, sleeping pills can provide temporary comfort when the emotions of anger (the urge to fight back) or of anxiety (the anticipation of danger) disturb sleep, but in time your brain will get accustomed to them, and you'll get addicted.

Think about those kids who are unfocused and underachieve in school. Many will concentrate better and gain (a chemical) focus from the stimulant drugs prescribed for ADD (attention deficit disorder—which is a woolly diagnosis at best). Did you know that a close chemical relative to these drugs is cocaine? Cocaine is known for its energy-giving high, and for its highly addictive quality. And what effect will long-term use have on the maturing brain? Would you volunteer your kids for that study?

Every time I try to look up the amount spent on prescription drugs for disordered emotions, I can never find a true number. Safe to say that billions of dollars are spent each year. By the time you read this sentence, the annual bill for psychotropic medication will be millions of dollars greater than it was when I wrote these words.

Prescription drugs, designed to calm, stimulate, tranquilize, and sedate the brain, are just as expensive as street drugs. The people who buy their drugs from a white-coated pharmacist in a neon-lit drugstore are seeking exactly the same emotional relief and sense of confident well-being as those who buy them in expensive zip-locked bags from furtive characters on dark street corners.

My drugstore in New York regularly delivers medication to my door when I am sick. In New York and other major cities, street drugs are delivered by couriers to the doorsteps or apartment lobbies of customers who have their dealers' secret numbers programmed into their cell phones.

All of these people are paying a high price, both financially and in terms of long-term health, for what I truly believe they are seeking—confidence—to live without the shame of self-criticism and the fear of others' disapproval, to respond calmly to life's normal reversals, and to be free of the haunting feelings of anxiety, anger, and self-pity. They want to feel confident in order to free themselves from these feelings, and to be able to take life's opportunities, for everyone has them. It is a challenge to play life's game with enthusiasm, courage, and determination, and you have a hand in how you perform.

Dr. Alex Comfort, in his book *The Nature of Human Nature*, wrote: "Man is the only animal which is inherently able, corporately and individually, to be his own worst enemy." Many people can relate to Dr. Comfort's statement. I like his name; I think "Sheenah Comfort" has a nice ring to it. The comfort I offer is of new ideas about how to build confidence and become your own best ally. Every one of us changes and adapts to new ideas all the time. I want you to change the way you manage your feelings. I know that if you take my psychological freedom drug, you will change and get to a position in your world that you can now only imagine. In the next chapter, I will write you a prescription for the Winning Hand of Comfort, the generic name for a drug you must take.

Let's be frank: "It is not only the separation between mind and brain that is mythical: the separation between mind and body is probably just as fictional," Antonio R. Damasio, *Descartes' Error: Emotion, Reason and the Human Brain*.

Let's be clear: Traumatized brains seek trauma, not comfort.

This chapter will answer three questions:

- Why do we all need calm and comfort?
- What do calm and comfort have to do with confidence?
- Why do so many brilliant people fool themselves into believing that something or someone can provide them with the calm and comfort they need?

WHY WE NEED CALM AND COMFORT

Imagine that you are walking along a deserted street in early winter. The sky is iron gray, and you feel that snow is coming. Suddenly, you hear a cry of distress and spot a small bundle lying on the sidewalk. Running toward it, you see a tiny baby wrapped in a thin blanket.

What is the first thing you would do after you gathered the infant into your arms and warmed it with your body heat inside your winter jacket? You, like all of us, would try to make sense of its desperate cries. What does this child want and need? Its mother and some milk—you know that this has to be true, but at this moment you cannot provide either. You call for help, and then you must wait until it arrives. And so you coo and calmly comfort the tiny frightened child. You speak to her softly and gently, promising her that you will take care of her. Perhaps you comfort her with a lullaby your mother once sang to you. You know the words; they are stored forever in your unconscious memory. You access them when your brain associates a child's distress with your need to comfort and calm that pain.

The tiny child does not know the meaning of words. She cannot yet understand your song of comfort, but she hears it and relaxes. Her cries become whimpers, and then she stops. She hears the rhythm and the voice tone, and her chaotic emotions settle back into a regular rhythm. Now she can look up at you and in her simple way just sense, just feel, that somehow she will survive.

The ambulance arrives and the infant is placed in the care of the local hospital. You are given a number to call to find out how she is. You walk on, pleased to be of use and with a story to tell. What you may not know is that you did far more than save a baby's life. You taught her something. You helped in the training of her brain, teaching it to associate fear and distress with the expectation of comfort and survival.

Our brains are designed to promote our survival. They are constantly on guard night and day. They must figure out ways to protect us and promote that survival. The tiny infant made a huge distress sound, and she survived because you associated that sound with a need for immediate help, and you responded.

It takes a long time for children to develop the neural connections between distress and the comfort that ensures survival. Only then will they realize that they will not be abandoned. Responsive parents help train their babies' brains every time they comfort them with their own particular words and songs, and with reassuring hugs and loving kisses. But they must do more. They need to present a comforting picture of the world by responding calmly to life's normal reversals: cuts and scrapes, friends who act cruelly, and everyday disappointments. They must be able to display their ability to calm and comfort themselves. They must not convey, through their own anxiety, that reasonable risks should not be taken, that normal reversals are someone else's fault and that they are awful. Instead, reversals are to be expected and one can quickly recover from the upset. And most of all, children must learn that other people are not mean and critical, but in general kind and cooperative. Most can be expected to step up to the plate if you are in *real* distress.

Did you grow up this way? I didn't, so my emotional reactions were immature for my age. I would overreact, dramatize, and complain when things went wrong (a normal reversal), and latch on to someone and something to blame as a way to stave off my own nasty self-critical habit. Better to feel self-pity than the shame of blaming myself. I did not even recognize that by blaming others and trying to induce them to feel guilt, I made myself look stupid and, of course, immature, as I damned them with faint logic. In railing against the heavens, I was nutty as Shakespeare's self-pitying King Lear, who cried, "I am a man more sinned against than sinning." Claiming that he was a hapless and helpless victim, Lear never realized that he was the engine of his eventual destruction.

In my younger years, I was unable to calm and comfort myself when I acted in ways that invited censure, and at other times I invented things to censure myself, even when nothing much was happening. When criticized I responded like a powerless child by raging, blaming, crying, and sulking, just like the vast majority of my clients. No one comforted me, because I was not a child. As a result of feeling deprived of well-deserved (in my firmly held opinion) sympathy, I got angrier.

Forced to leave the safe zone of my mother's side when I went to university, I felt scared and exposed, and hid away from everyone. I slipped into depression. My overloaded brain shut me down—told me to shut up for my own psychological protection. I cut classes, I developed illnesses, and I stayed home. I almost failed.

In the limbic system of my brain, unbeknownst to me, the chemical components designed to calm me down lay dormant. Similar in effect to morphine, they work for all of us when our overstressed brains require our help. As in the case of all good drugs, just knowing that they are in the medicine cabinet is a beginning, but we must open the vial and take them in order to calm the pain we feel.

The limbic system is an area of the brain that interacts between our basic instincts to survive and experiences gained from our environment. We humans, throughout our lives, automatically balance and regulate everything in our brain and body: food intake and bowel and bladder output; we put on a sweater or turn on an air conditioner—we just know when our body temperature is unbalanced and we feel stressed.

An overstressed brain will panic; it will obsess and ruminate. It will be unstable and easily enraged. Fear will paralyze it and many people will slip down the dark spiral to depression, which at its most severe is a response to too much mental exhaustion. For the seriously depressed, the effort required to simply get out of bed to brush one's teeth can feel as difficult as setting forth on a crusade. In order to regulate this dark and hopeless emotional state, you must strive to right the imbalance. You have the treatment necessary within your complex brain chemistry. You need to free yourself from the emotional prisons that bar you from competing in your world with calm confidence.

The next short paragraphs are directed at people who are seriously depressed and may have a genetic propensity for various types of depression. These include episodes of what are properly called "major depression" and "bipolar disorder" (more commonly known as manic depression). These paragraphs are short because the number of sufferers is very low when statistically compared to the general population. These remarks do *not* apply to the vast majority of readers (some of whom may have been misdiagnosed as depressed), but here are my concerns for the few:

1. Be sure, absolutely sure, that you fit the diagnostic criteria. (Look them up and check for yourself. *The Diagnostic and Statistical Manual* of the American Psychiatric Association is available in bookstores and on the Internet.) Do not accept a casual diagnosis. If someone, even a doctor, says, "You're depressed," it does not necessarily mean that you fit the criteria for a serious depressive disorder. Always get a second, and even a third opinion. Remember, doctors give you opinions, not absolute facts.

2. Make certain that you fully understand the long-term side effects of any drug prescribed for you. Choosing the correct drug and the correct dosage is central and important, and an expert can change both to offer you the most protection possible. Dr. Jesse Rosenthal, a highly regarded psychopharmacologist in New York City, told me that prescribing psychotropic medication is as much an art as it is a science. Training and especially experience are needed to select the best prescription in the right dosage taken at the right time of day for each individual.

3. Do not accept at face value the TV and print-ad campaigns from drug manufacturers. These marketing tools are about money, not your health. They overstate the case in terms of how many people can be accurately diagnosed and how effective the medication is. For example, no pill can cure social anxiety, as the advertisements

imply. A pill can calm you down, but there is no chemical pre-scription for confidence.

4. Do *not* hide behind an erroneous or fuzzy diagnosis. You will spend your life meandering miserably through the meadows of medication at an enormous cost to your bank balance (or insurance premiums) and your health.

If you truly have an accurately diagnosed emotional or thought disorder and are receiving the proper treatment, you most definitely need to learn to calm and comfort yourself in order to face your illness confidently. Your brain needs your help. It has been proven over and over again that a confident, positive attitude helps all who are sick to make the best of their lives, and many will live far longer than expected. Put your hands over both of your ears and gently hold your skull. Your hands are covering the emotional control centers of your brain. These are the areas that need your calm and comforting hands, when they are overloaded with painful feelings.

COMFORT FOR ADULTS

Short of a major crisis we adults must not depend on or rely on others for comfort. We will eventually avoid the phone calls and the company of others who do. Knowing how to manage emotions is not an innate ability, but an essential survival operation that requires skills we must learn and practice over and over again. Humans have a very long period in which to develop maturity. Unlike chimpanzees, our nearest relative, we are not actually able to reproduce until our early teens, and then we are mostly prevented from doing so, as teenagers are considered too immature to handle the responsibility of parenthood.

During these years, we acquire a myriad of skills, both practical and psychological, which prepare us to deal competently with the world. Sadly, many people miss out on developing the ability to moderate their emotions, because their parents missed out, too. In extreme emotional circumstances, such as real and objective danger, the brain bypasses the thinking centers and makes a decision based purely on emotion. These responses are known as fight, flight, or freeze. You will rage in anger or run away in terror, or you will freeze, rabbitlike, in the headlights, hoping your quiet, compliant stance will influence your tormentor to retreat. In extreme circumstances, when your life is threatened, this is how you respond—you are programmed—it is not a choice, but an emotional decision. Except in serious situations, emotional decisions are almost always a very bad idea. All crimes of passion are emotional decisions, as are all acts of foolhardy anger, like road rage. Avoidance and procrastination are emotional decisions based on anxiety.

In an interview on National Public Radio, the Hollywood producer Robert Evans told a story about problems he faced in trying to get *The Godfather* movie into production. The movie's backers were extremely anxious. They had three major concerns: a Mafia movie was unlikely to be popular; Marlon Brando was the wrong actor to play the lead; the movie would be too long and not hold the audience's attention. Had Evans acted on these anxious predictions of failure, millions of people would have been denied the pleasure of seeing a significant movie and a much imitated performance by a brilliant actor. Asked how so many experienced experts could be so off base with their predictions, Evans replied, "Few people know about anything." Cool reason trumps overheated emotions.

In order to make good decisions, it is essential to calm down a little at first. Children are not expected to be so wise; adults are. The whole process of stimulating and retraining your brain for freedom from excessive emotion is an essential skill that everyone must acquire in order to be free to live the confident life and play with a Winning Hand.

I often imagine what life was like for early humans. Living in simple villages, they survived in an almost empty world. There were so few people and so many animals to hunt, and fruit and berries to gather from abundant vegetation. Yet life was not necessarily simpler for early humans than for those of us surviving in cities and suburban developments, or in the small country towns and farming hamlets that define the U.S.A. We hunt for salaries and wages, and we forage through supermarkets, country stores, and corner bodegas for our supplies.

What do we have in common with early humans? Almost everything. In order to survive, the early humans would have been as wary about leaving the security of their village to venture after game and to scavenge the carcasses of prey killed by larger predators as we are when we travel on city subways or walk alone on dark country roads.

Early humans mostly stayed in safe walking distance from home base. As climates improved, many would decide to make the long journey northward. Without much information, they moved to unknown places. Today, people often move from town to town, state to state, or across the world, leaving the familiarity of what they know. It takes courage to leave the security of the familiar. What is courage? The answer is simple but often overlooked: Courage is the ability to calm and comfort the anxiety that erupts when we look to the future and predict what dire events might occur. As early humans sharpened their weapons and packed their supplies, they must have calmed their fears and confidently believed that they could succeed on this journey of no return.

I can imagine the grief of the people left behind. They would have wept as they saw their family members becoming smaller and smaller as they moved toward the horizon. I can also imagine that some who remained behind were elderly and infirm. Others who stayed at home lacked the confidence to believe that a better life with more resources and the satisfaction of high achievement were even possible. We should all be grateful to those who did venture forth, because every one of us is here today as a result. As a gesture of thanks to our brave and confident ancestors, let me suggest that you learn to apply the Winning Hand of Comfort to your disruptive and disabling feelings, and free yourself from the self-doubting anxiety that undermines your courage and creativity.

WHAT CALM AND COMFORT HAVE TO DO WITH CONFIDENCE

In a study conducted by John Guttman and Bernardo Carducci and published in *Psychology Today*, the authors reported the startling statistic that 47 percent of Americans are shy or socially anxious. It cannot be that almost half the population is *born* shy. Shyness handicaps all and disables many, mostly because it makes it very hard to ask for help. Imagine a shy person asking friends and family for a loan to help them start a business or buy a house, or making a sexual move and once in bed maintaining an erection or having an orgasm. It can be done, but the emotional cost is high, and many will never ask and will make do with far less.

I know, as do you, that some humans are born with a trait to be quiet and contemplative. Others have noisier, more outgoing temperaments. This works well for human survival. We need all of our diverse inherited differences in order to work creatively to reinvent and improve our lives. This is why throughout history great seaports that welcomed newcomers from different countries and cultures became innovative, profitable, and successful. All humans are brilliant and to some degree different. We are all designed to promote the common good—to enhance progress, to promote survival. Yet, I truly believe that most of us lack confidence and as a result are underachievers. We have far more to offer than we feel we can give. And our feelings, not our abilities, are the problem.

Harold Macmillan, the hoary former prime minister of the United Kingdom, was gifted with a dry wit. When asked what a leader fears, his often quoted reply was, "Events, dear boy, events." When fear of "events" prevents us from believing that we can survive and succeed efficiently, and when we are stalled by the anxiety of potential failure, we are making negative predictions based on our feelings. I tease some of my clients by pointing out that they think they are fortune-tellers. They peer into a glass darkly and see danger and devastation in the future. They could never make any money with a crystal ball and a Gypsy storefront, because to earn a living fortune-tellers must offer more hope than hopelessness. Some accuse me of being overly optimistic—a pathological optimist. Like litigating attorneys, they will offer me so-called evidence to prove that I am wrong in not joining them in their negativity promoted by a habit of self-pitying anxiety:

- "I lose my erection so often—how could I ever please a woman?"
- "I got fired from my job. What makes you think I can ever get another or keep it if I could?"
- "My mother is impossible. I love her, but she does nothing but criticize me or give me dumb advice. She makes me feel so insecure and indecisive. She won't change."
- "I got divorced. My husband left me, and you tell me I should like and trust men!"

People will go to tremendous and irrational lengths to try to prove to me and to themselves that to be anxious is normal. They feel and believe that their feelings are about reality. Some go further and tell me that worrying ahead of time is a preventative—a prophylactic that you pop on to keep you out of trouble.

Anxiety should only be felt in the presence of a serious threat or potential danger. The threat must be real, not just psychological. Fortunately, few of us will face this kind of threat, and we hold those who do, such as policemen, troops in combat, firefighters, combat pilots, and all people of courage, in the highest regard. But even these front-line heroes must calm and comfort themselves enough to think clearly, so that they can climb the ladder into the blazing building or land the fighter jet on the deck of the aircraft carrier on a dark and stormy night.

To be nervous occasionally, such as when you face a job interview, a blind date, or a performance of some kind, is normal. Baseball and football coaches incite just enough nervousness in their players to enhance focus and performance: "Come on, guys. Go for it. Get out there and beat 'em." To be fearful regularly is not normal.

When I think of freedom, I remember the angry, self-conscious young woman who bore my name but whom I no longer know very well. She (I) was trapped with self-critical shame and helpless self-pity. Today I am mostly free of her, but I know she still dwells in my brain; I sometimes hear her timid, oh-so-critical voice when it filters through from time to time. Right now she is casting doubts on this enterprise: "Will anyone buy this book that you have devoted so much time to and value so much? I bet your life's work ends up on the discount rack, slammed by the critics as a bunch of vapid psychobabble. Will you be a loser? Will anyone benefit from your experience? I doubt it. Shouldn't you stop now and spend your weekends having fun? Go on, go shopping, hang out with your husband, cook and garden, visit your friends. Your vacations are mostly spent writing this dumb book— that's not a vacation. Relax. You work too hard. Hard work makes us dull. Pamper yourself—you deserve it."

As a wave of anxiety and self-pity gathers strength, I feel a change beginning in my brain. It calms down. The wave has lost its energy and ebbs away before I give in to despair and procrastination. My retrained brain has calmed and comforted me, and I can proceed.

I know I will only feel free from shame and self-criticism if I do what I believe is right. I want to make a difference in the world. You will not succeed unless you, too, retrain your brain to calm and comfort itself, so that you can think clearly and make decisions based on good judgment and not on emotions.

So, what do you associate with the word "freedom"? Sit quietly for a moment and ask your brain: What do I think of when I say the word "freedom"? Add the word "psychological" to the mix. What would it be like to be psychologically free?

How about freedom from ever feeling stupid, or feeling (or being) fat? Would you like to stop feeling old, even if you are in your advanced years? How about ugly—freedom from that self-absorbed criticism would make you feel more attractive. Feeling like a loser is like wallowing in a pit of shame.

What else are people supposed to do when they suffer from emotional immaturity and look outward for comfort? Many who are so strong and independent in certain key areas of their lives in fact rely on substances to calm down: alcohol, which quickly injects itself into the bloodstream, and satisfying foods like milky ice cream, which has the consistency of baby food. Sugars metabolize fast and give us a high—a mood elevation for a while. Put chocolate and caffeine together and you get a double shot. If you comfort yourself with food, there will soon just be more of you to try to comfort.

Others have more threatening and even dangerous ways of seeking calm and comfort—gamblers and those who shop incessantly and spend beyond their means. People who get high by repeated sexual conquest. Those that rely on street drugs to kill fear and silence self-pity and shame.

On the evening news and in gossip columns we often hear a similar story. Some celebrity has fallen from grace due to booze or drugs or crazy sexual rampages. How can this be? we ask, he or she had it all. You now know that the person's feelings were the problem, and his or her means of so-called comfort and calm had become an addiction.

Repeated binges are always an immature way to seek temporary calm and quiet from painful feelings. Only immature children need and can expect external emotional support. The rest of us can expect support from our underwear. Emotionally, support is up to us. To be in command of our emotions means living without a constant repetitive urge to binge. It means freedom from the self-defeating traps we daily set for ourselves.

Would you like to be free from your guilty habit of pleasing others, without discomfort? How about freedom from overreacting to criticism? Does that appeal? I know well and continue to relish the feeling of freedom from procrastination.

Confidence means doing everything that you fear, and for people who are socially shy this is the freedom to step into the center of the crowd and comfortably enjoy the sunlight of social connection. This is what the Winning Hand of Comfort will provide.

When Mark Twain wrote, "I've seen troubles in my life. Luckily most of them never occurred," he was referring to his negative feelings. So many of us are trapped in feelings that only feel real. Let's change all that with the drug of Freedom.

SEVEN

THE WINNING HAND OF COMFORT

A DRUG CALLED FREEDOM

"What color is it?"

"Green," I replied. I was referring to the nasty gunk in my lungs that was limiting my breathing and causing intense bouts of coughing. I was responding to a question from Ray, my internist, whose wisdom I trust. Green meant that herds of migrating germs were galloping by the millions through the swamplands in my chest.

"Antibiotics," Ray said.

"Okay," I said. "I really want to feel better. The bugs are winning."

Now it is my turn to prescribe for you. I will write a prescription for the drug of Freedom that will forever change the way you feel about yourself and the world. You will need to take it regularly and follow all of the protocols. Like Ray, I can promise results. You will soon feel better.

Excessive germs in our bodies create generalized sickness. Excessive amounts of feelings create sickness, too—both mental and, at times, physical.

I have designed a new drug. It will have no side effects. When I chose a name for it I did not decide on some strange new word stuffed with consonants, but lean on vowels, that refuses to trip off the tongue. The drug companies like to invent titles from the lineage of biotechnology. Even though the therapeutic effects of my drug are entirely biochemical, like all of our feelings, I chose something simpler— a word you know and must never forget. I call it "Freedom."

The name implies Freedom from anxiety and fear; Freedom from shame and immature anger; Freedom from the self-pity that promotes passivity; Freedom from the catchall label "depression" that is so much a fad at this point in our cultural evolution. This is what the drug of Freedom will provide. Like many of the well-known anti-anxiety and antidepressant treatments, it will not work at first—it will take time.

You yourself must administer the psychological drug Freedom. Unlike other medications, Freedom is an inside job. If you were taught to respond honestly and calmly to life's normal reversals and were comforted during the few but painful major crises all people must face, do not read on. However, you most likely know plenty of people whom this book, and especially this chapter, could kick-start on the path toward maturity and the confidence called Freedom.

It is much more likely that you do need to learn how to activate, and in fact retrain, your brain to calm, comfort, manage, and moderate your feelings. If this is so, we will proceed together.

Let's be frank: Traumatized brains seek trauma.

Let's be clear: Like a nagging toothache, untreated feelings cannot be ignored.

When someone asks me, "How are you feeling?" I usually reply, "I'm fine." I really don't know what else to say because I am usually not really feeling much at all. The ability to spend my day without paying much attention to myself and my feelings is a freedom that for so many years I did not know existed.

Only when I was faced with a crisis of my own making was I forced to set aside my internal emotional life and respond maturely. I had been lost in an emotional construction site—a place where I had crafted defenses against what I believed was a critical world out to prove to me that I was a stupid, fat loser. It looked pretty stupid to have ended up alone on my mother's doorstep with four kids in need of shelter. I looked like a real loser, but when anyone dared to imply that I, the innocent one, was the cause of my own downfall, I would explode in blame and fury, and, Learlike, rail at life and all the forces beyond my control that were the cause of my family's troubles.

Fortunately, I had little time to indulge in my self-pitying, enraged misery. I had to make money, for the boys' feet seemed to grow daily and shoes cost a fortune. Boys' clothes I could find in second-hand stores. I would wash and mend them, and my guys never knew that they once belonged to other kids. The headmaster of the boys' school handed down two worn but respectable uniforms that helped a lot. But shoes must fit and must be new. (Today, shoes have a special meaning for me because I can now afford them, and I buy lots of them—high heels in all colors, summer sandals, winter boots, and rubber gardening shoes. I love them all.)

I learned that when I calmed down I had the energy and could make the effort necessary to take care of my boys and myself. The brain makes up just 3 percent of the tissue mass of the human body, yet it uses 30 percent of the body's glucose—the fuel that energizes and runs the body. Emotional overload is draining. All the energy I had wasted complaining I now needed to move forward. I wrote myself a job review at that time:

Deficits: Immature (very!): Wanted to be provided for and taken care of—complained angrily when partner failed to do so. Resented authority. Tried to please everyone, to have them like me and never criticize me—instead turned into a resentful, self-pitying pleaser. Confidence (none!): No belief that I could take care of myself and make enough money. Self-critical (very!): Stupid, fat, loser, unsexy—no man would want me, especially with four kids. In a childlike fashion, I was always comparing myself to others and losing.

Assets: children (4), college degree (just), postgraduate qualification (yes), health (excellent), personality (pleasant and fun-loving when not self-pitying), work ethic (Scottish puritan background—excellent, when not procrastinating). Result: Stop complaining and go, girl!

It was time to build confidence and to assist my brain on its natural path to emotional maturity. I want you to ask yourself: How do I feel? I want your answer to be *fine*, and I want this to be true most of the time. When you do face life's normal reversals, I want you to be able to manage your feelings maturely, so that you can deal effectively and easily with the inevitable obstacles that pop up in our lives. For life is not difficult; we just make it that way.

THE BRAIN RETRAINING PROGRAM: A PRESCRIPTION FOR FREEDOM FROM EMOTIONAL PAIN

The Winning Hand of Comfort is a brain-retraining program. With persistence and practice, you will permanently reshape the neural pathways in your plastic, ever-maturing brain. Your brain is aware and listening. As you listen to me, your brain is questioning and connecting the thought of Freedom with past memories and experiences. Freedom—every Fourth of July in the U.S.A. we celebrate freedom from British rule. My parents connected the word with freedom from Nazi oppression at the end of World War II.

The famed journalist George Will, speaking on the ABC television program *This Week,* remarked, "Many people feel irrationally entitled to a risk-free life." Yet, most so-called risks occur not in life, but in our imaginations. Perceptions and predictions drive pessimistic fears of damage to our person or to our self-respect, and so we undermine our confidence.

We create shameful and embarrassing scenes in our brains. Many imagine themselves as potential victims in a dangerous world. They, for example, refuse to fly, ride in elevators, or go to parties. Shame, self-pity, anxiety, and anger rise to a level that each of us has learned to live with and to expect. Secure in this familiar emotional bind, we are unaware that we tie ourselves down with images, thoughts, and actions, including inactions, that take us back to our emotional home base. We call up scenes to generate these feelings. We act in a private play we have created in our brains, a play designed to generate feelings we know so well and hate so much. Now is the time to begin to change.

FREEDOM: THE WINNING HAND OF COMFORT

The five fingers: Calm, Clarify, Challenge, Comfort, Confidence

Calm: Finger One points out that you need to calm down just a little in order to think clearly. Fortunately, this is not too difficult. Anger and anxiety are fast-acting emotions. They come on quickly and can cool down as quickly. You will need to reduce anger and anxiety just enough to clear your brain and avoid an emotional decision; luckily, an overstressed brain is designed to act fast with no time to think. It must get you out of trouble, pronto.

Say, "I will calm down and think" three times. Breathe very slowly. Each time say this simple sentence: "I—will—calm—down—and—think." Now pause and close your eyes; you will note that you feel a very slight trickle-down of chemically charged calm through your neural pathways. Your brain is listening. A tiny amount of this drug I call Freedom is being released and is being injected into your bloodstream. With your ongoing help, Freedom will begin its journey, transported in your blood, and begin to infuse your tense body with a sense of comforting calm.

Clarify: Finger Two reminds you that it is time to put your finger on the facts. Now that your brain is beginning to clear you are able to clarify exactly what you are feeling.

Let's begin with *anxiety*. Ask yourself two questions:

The Winning Hand of Comfort

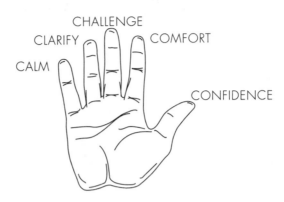

CHALLENGE
CLARIFY   COMFORT
CALM
CONFIDENCE

CALM
Calm yourself a bit by breathing slowly.
Tell yourself to calm down.
In seconds your brain will clear just enough for you to think.

CLARIFY
Clarify your thinking.
Ask: Am I angry? Go deeper. Ask: What am I feeling ashamed/ humiliated about? Now you can recognize your shame habit. And/or ask: Am I feeling anxious? Go deeper. Ask: What am I feeling sorry for myself about? (Feeling helpless or hopeless) Now you can recognize your self-pity habit.

CHALLENGE
Challenge your thinking.
Ask: What am I blaming myself for? (Creating shame)
Ask: What am I blaming others misfortune or the world for? (Creating self-pity)
Reframe your thoughts without blame. Write them down if this helps.

COMFORT
Comforting your feelings is the key to confidence.
Repeat over and over again your preferred words of comfort. Say the same words every time.
Write your comfort phrase here:

Do this until you physically feel the drug of Freedom begin to calm your brain, freeing it from high levels of anger and anxiety.
Never miss an opportunity to practice this until you have created an automatic comfort habit.

CONFIDENCE
You will think clearly, act wisely, and never make emotional decisions.
You will be free of reactive anger and anxiety, living in the world and not locked in an emotionally overloaded brain.
The drug of Freedom flows freely, coming automatically to your aid when you are upset.

- Am I feeling scared, fearful, and anxious?
- Does my behavior indicate that I am anxious? (For example, avoidance, procrastination, passive pleasing, compulsive tidying, and bingeing.)

Now let's check out *anger*. Ask yourself the obvious questions: Am I feeling angry? Most of us do not need to ask this question. We feel the heat of anger in our bodies, and want to act in punitive ways. We may slam doors, drive less well than normal, shout or sulk, or simply be irritable with everyone. Others do *not* realize that they are mad. For them, it is too shameful or risky to show or even feel anger. Many people do not recognize anger, but mistake it for anxiety. They are wolves in sheep's clothing—on the surface they appear passive, timid, compliant, and agreeable, when it seems clear that they are being treated in ways that would anger most of us. They, too, will act in punitive ways to others. They will often be late and forgetful, withdrawn and self-involved, or unenthusiastic and definitely uninterested in sex. Many will act punitively toward themselves by bingeing and immaturely refusing to take care of themselves.

Question your behavior. If you act in any of these ways, if you often feel depressed, if you please others too much and complain internally, if you often get sick and feel sorry for yourself, you are angry. Please believe me. You are angry.

And now for the bigger challenge. Having clarified the reactive emotions of anger and anxiety (reactions to a threat, either real or imagined), you now face the task of what lies beneath. What powerful and strongly felt currents are churning up these waves of anger or those tides of anxiety?

Unless you answer this question with *clarity*, you cannot proceed with your brain retraining prescription.

The real culprits lie beneath the surface: the turbulence of anger and the timidity of anxiety. These emotions are freely felt and often expressed, yet they are anchored to more chronic immature emotions that belong in the bedrock of our pasts. They are shame and self-pity.

Footnote on self-pity—be wary. Many of my clients refuse to believe that they have a self-pity habit even if they binge and whine, please, avoid and procrastinate, complain, and blame. Why? Because they are so intrinsically self-critical that to acknowledge a self-pity habit would be a new branch of hurtful criticism to add to the bonfire of shame that smolders their confidence away.

Let's be frank: Giving up criticizing, complaining, and blaming is shedding a protective coating that you do not need.

Let's be clear: Self-pity is the strangler fig around the tree of life.

Challenge: Finger Three. Raise your third finger and bend the others down. Jerk your erect finger upward toward your brain. Repeat several times. If you are uncomfortable with making rude gestures, do it anyway. Do what you fear.

You are now physically and wordlessly insulting yourself. You are treating yourself as a disgusting person who deserves ill treatment—someone who deserves to be disrespected. If you look around you in a crowd of people, you can assume that though they are behaving normally, many of them are criticizing and insulting themselves internally: "You jerk! You loser! You stupid, fat, old, ugly loser!"

To be confident one must firmly believe in one's ability to survive and succeed. This requires encouragement and reassurance when facing a challenge, big or small. It also means being able to calm and comfort oneself with a quick injection of Freedom from fear when anxiety arises and when others criticize and diminish your efforts.

For so many, the opposite is true. Instead, they refer to stored exhibits of past embarrassments and humiliating events in their personal Museums of Shame. They revisit these symbols of shame and failure every time a compliment, a hopeful opportunity, or an important challenge comes their way. They also make regular trips to these Halls of Criticism and relive past failures as if these inevitably predict the future. They may presume that no one can ever change.

Thoughts feed and sustain feelings, and if we act on our feelings, we are ignoring the experience and sage wisdom stored in our prefrontal cortex. This part of the brain is the center of intellect and reasoning, our own personal computer. It is not my purpose here to explain how this functions. Suffice to say, as with the big gray box that sits on my office desk, understanding its inner workings are not as important to me as knowing how to operate it effectively. It would be tough to write this book without my gray and mostly cooperative assistant.

Your cerebral computer is mostly cooperative, too. It will rhythmically repeat the programs installed into its hard drive in a feedback loop called an "algorithm." This information is a form of propaganda. Repetition encourages belief.

My client Anne claimed she came from the wrong side of the tracks. "We were nobodies. My father owned a bar that was a bit notorious. In school my friends looked down on me." Shame was a constant and familiar feeling generated in her family by this "nobodies from the wrong side of the tracks" way of thinking.

Anne went to college, married a great guy, had two children, and maintained a responsible job. She and her husband worked hard and created financial stability. They had recently bought a fine home in a great school district. Surprisingly, Anne was miserable and depressed, and her friends insisted that she see me.

"What am I doing moving to this neighborhood? No one will like me. They will think I am stupid and low class."

Anne continued her self-denigration until I stopped her. "Please stop. This is hard to hear. It is also a really self-centered way to think."

Anne blanched and her mouth fell open. "What, me? Self-centered? I spend my life doing things for others."

"I am sure you are kind," I replied. "Humans are inherently kind. But you are trying to buy approval—to overcome your shameful feelings." I pointed out to Anne that it is self-centered to make up what others will think of us, and it is not kind to please others just for their approval. She was feeding her shame habit, and that had nothing to do with her neighbors or their potential opinions. I went on to show Anne how her thoughts cause and nurture her miserable shame, and how these are habits learned in her past. She had to challenge them. You need to, also.

Here is how Anne challenged her shameful thoughts. After she had calmed down a little and clarified her chronic feelings, she could go to the audiotape in her thinking brain. Anne recognized her shame habit. She pinpointed three thoughts or beliefs that drove her into shame, which in turn generated anxiety and her desire to avoid her neighbors:

- "I am a stupid person. I was never a great student, and I am low class, too. This makes me unacceptable and likely to be rejected."
- "I am fat. This makes me unacceptable."
- "I am a loser—that is who I am."

I asked Anne to challenge her beliefs, but she resisted my efforts at first because her three beliefs *felt* real to her. Finally, she was able to question them a little. She challenged her thinking and wrote out revised opinions. She found that carrying these newly thought-out statements in her wallet helped her to rehearse. When she slipped into her old familiar thinking patterns she would take out her notes and read her challenges:

- "I am stupid and low class, too. This makes me unacceptable." Given that Anne tried but could not prove to me that she was stupid, and could find no one to agree with this emotional conclusion, she understood that calling herself "low class" was her family's way of feeling ashamed. "*Shame. It is just my way of thinking. I can change that,*" she wrote.
- "I am fat. This makes me unacceptable." This statement became, "*I could lose a few pounds, but that will not happen un-*

til I fix my shame habit, because feeling fat gives me an excuse to feel shame." When Anne stopped comparing herself to a very thin friend, she recognized that she used comparisons to shame herself. She made a decision, *I can be more attractive. I will focus on doing everything I can to be as attractive as possible.*

- "I am a loser" became, *"My parents felt a lot of loser shame. I do not have to carry on that familiar feeling in my life and infect my children with my habit.* In reality, Mom and Dad raised three kids. We always had a home and food on the table. I am better off financially than my parents, and I will counter my shameful thinking and be better off emotionally."

Every time you feel hurtful, painful feelings, I encourage you to write down the three most common thoughts that fire up your shame engine and challenge them. Carry these new statements with you. Look for what is familiar, and never forget that the root of the word "familiar" is family.

When Anne had truly rehearsed and could put the Winning Hand of Comfort into practice, she understood what I meant by the word "Freedom." She was mostly free from her hostile habit of raging when her husband or children disagreed with her or pointed out an error she had made. She could now react calmly and maturely. She was also free to mingle with her new neighbors, knowing she, not they, had been the judgmental critic.

Let us return to self-pity and the rhythmic, often repeated thoughts that drive it. Pick the top three most prevalent thoughts that conjure up your feelings of self-pity. Note the helpless, passive tone these thoughts have. Here are three of mine that have lost a lot of their power to make me feel victimized:

- Poor me. I am the only girl in a family of four. Boys and men have it easy.

- I am not attractive and sexy enough. Why can't I have a better body and straight hair?
- I did well in school, but my mother told me that it was because I worked hard. I am not really smart.

These immature and helpless statements haunted me for much of my young adult life. I challenged them long ago, and now they create just ripples of occasional dissatisfaction. My thinking was inaccurate—not at all realistic. In my family, the boys did have it easier. But as adults, my brothers seemed even less confident than I did. (My brothers Grant and Peter died, and will never get to read this book. I wish I could change that. When I think of them, I feel very sad.)

I did change the way I thought and felt about my body. Fortunately, several men have found me both sexy and attractive, and my husband still does. I decided that I own my body. This is where I live. Therefore I will decorate it, dress it well, keep it fit, and respect it.

So, now you understand the challenge. Again, let me remind you of your commitment to complete all the tasks I ask of you. Never act impulsively on your emotions. Instead, address them and when provoked, take time to calm and clarify your feelings and challenge your thinking. Practice this method repeatedly in order to retrain the thinking center of your brain. Be persistent.

Comfort: Finger Four. For those who lack confidence, comfort is a foreign language. Criticism is their native tongue, and when speaking another, they mispronounce it and don't know very much vocabulary. This is quite normal, yet shame-filled critics will call themselves *stupid* if they stumble over the words when they try to comfort themselves. But persistence is inherent in all of us. Never say, "I can't do this comforting business"—challenge yourself to succeed instead.

The practice of using their biochemical ability to regulate their emotional thermostat separates out confident, mature, fully functional, forward-thinking adults who play life's game with a Winning Hand. Left behind are the others, whose confidence and contribution to the common good are stifled and, in some cases, strangled by immature emotional habits. The old-fashioned term "neurotic" is often applied to them. The current psychobabble way to describe them is to say they "have issues," a phrase I dislike just as much as "neurotic."

To calm and comfort our feelings, we must find the words that appeal directly to our emotional habits—shame and self-pity—that drive our anxiety and anger when a threat is not actual but imagined (perceived). Catchwords, clichés, sound bites, proverbs, platitudes, aphorisms, affirmations, mantras, homilies, and oft-repeated sayings all have a singular purpose: They are meant to promote a common truth and influence the listener or reader to join in a communal belief, even if it is an assumption, a bias, or an opinion that lacks merit.

If we hear these words often enough, we will automatically store them in our unconscious long-term memory. They will rhythmically return to our consciousness when our brain associates the phrase with a current event. It is quite possible to brainwash people with repeated familiar statements of belief. All parents, and influential others like schoolteachers and religious leaders, "brainwash" children to some degree by repeating commonly held assumptions. Some are plain common sense—if I say "You can't take it with you," no further explanation is necessary.

I contend that most of these overused statements are not so clearly true. They are deemed to be so, and they rise like a fashionable trend, only to evaporate when they no longer seem relevant. Two of the so-called truths I want to help fade away are the notion of our needing "self-esteem," as in self-admiration because of who one is and not what one does. Second, the popular notion that "people don't change" (implying that *you* can't change) is bandied about without thought. We are all in a constant state of adaptation, and we all know people who have changed. As you read this, your brain is listening and questioning. It is changing right now.

The language of comfort is a phrase or sentence that you will create to become your own influential statement. It must be repeated every time you need to manage your emotions. I cannot give you these words, for as with comforting music, you must select language that appeals to you and to your sensibility.

Words are just a construction of alphabet letters, empty shells that we stuff with personal meaning. In time, your comfort phrase will become so familiar to you that it will actually lose its meaning and become an effective symbol only. You will instantly recognize that you must comfort yourself and calm down. Your brain will respond in a nanosecond. It will know what you wish for, and your wish will be granted before you finish your sentence.

Here is my personal comfort phrase: "Sheenah, don't overreact." As a former histrionic given to loud complaining and temper tantrums, this phrase works well for me. As I write this down, my brain is responding. I can feel a mild anesthetic streaming through my neural pathways. I can physically feel the fluids trickle down.

The drug Freedom will not turn you into a drugged-down and compliant passenger in life, for that would have no survival potential. Instead, it will free you from anxiety, fear, irritability, and irrational anger most of the time. Apply it after the initial investigation into exactly what your feelings are, and how your thoughts and actions are feeding them.

Unlike many of the excellent medications my good doctor keeps in his little black bag, Freedom will not work very fast. Your attempt at applying a comforting statement will seem like a meaningless and even silly device at first. But in a sense, these strung-together words are not so much about their intrinsic meaning, for any preferred proverb from "God is love," to "Get off your own back" would do the same job. What we are striving for here is a *structure*—a reminder, a title, or a description that signals calm and comfort, and a return to a steady state.

Our brains arouse themselves in response to our interpretations and evaluations of an event. At each step in this thinking process we are moving farther away from the facts of the event and deeper into our personal beliefs and familiar emotional states.

For example, my client Harry reported that his manager had walked right past him without greeting him. At first, Harry simply thought that the woman was in a great hurry and could not spare the time to acknowledge him. As he thought more about it, he began to reevaluate what had happened, and felt increasingly angry: "What a bitch! She must be dissatisfied with my performance and is too cowardly to tell me to my face."

His mood darkened as he assumed that he would never get ahead in this world. By now he was in a familiar state of shame, self-pity, and resentment, and his thinking increased this emotional connection to his past. "I am such a f——g loser," he thought, and he generated more and more shame and self-pity, anger and anxiety. Mistakenly believing his feelings to be reality, Harry was about to make an emotional decision that would have made his life difficult.

Later in the day, Harry, his colleagues, and boss gathered in a corridor outside a conference room for a scheduled meeting. Harry was determined to keep quiet. "Why share my ideas with her? She doesn't value me. I am going nowhere fast." As he stood grimly and self-centeredly, lost in his self-pity and anger, he was startled when he felt a tap on his arm.

"Harry, was that you I passed on the street?" his boss asked. "I thought I saw you from the corner of my eye. I'm sorry if I ignored you, but I was so caught up in my worry and concerns about this meeting. I'm sure that you have some ideas to help with our current situation. You always do."

Harry and his boss had much in common. Harry's overaroused brain had responded in his familiar way and set him angrily apart from her. She had unwittingly saved him from a self-defeating maneuver for which he would have blamed her for the rest of his life, but she had intervened. Without knowing it, she had comforted him.

Harry was sorely in need of the Winning Hand of Comfort. He had often made decisions based on the emotions of the moment. These had blighted his ambition and damaged relationships. When I urged him to find a comfort phrase, he found one that suited him well. He chose "Calm down and think." In time it worked for him. As he persistently applied his personal comfort phrase, Harry ceased to be a self-appointed victim of his formerly inaccurate assumptions and miserable feelings.

Let's be frank: You *can* teach an old dog new tricks. They learn faster when they realize that the old tricks don't work.

Let's be clear: It's crazy not to talk to yourself—with your personal comfort phrase.

I am always fascinated by the comfort language my clients select. Here are some recent samples:

- This feeling is temporary.
- Calm down. It's no big deal.
- Come on. You don't have to feel this way.

A writer composed a poetic line: "Let the sun rise in my brain." An avid reader of Jane Austen took a quotation from *Pride and Prejudice*, "I will be mistress of my feelings." A musician took a title from a much loved song: "With a Song in My Heart." In contrast, my own— "Sheenah, don't overreact"—seems very plain and Scottish puritanical, but the statement works for me, now in an automatic, even magical way.

However, the words themselves are not the central issue. The *structure* of the phrase and the constant repetition will take you far beyond their original meaning. Your brain will abstract the message—comfort, calm, and prepare you to think about what you need to do.

We will never really know how past heroes and heroines who confidently played life's game with great success calmed their turbulent feelings. How did Winston Churchill calm himself down enough to wage war on a fearsome and powerful enemy? Perhaps his comfort phrase is embedded in the very first speech he gave to the House of Commons on May 13, 1940. In his measured, booming voice he said,

"What is our aim? I can answer in one word. Victory! Victory at all costs, victory in spite of all terror, victory however long and hard the road may be: for without victory there is no survival." It appears to me that his comfort phrase was a single word: victory!

It will be a victory for you when, with persistence and practice, your comfort phrase will become scaffolding set firmly in place to support your shaky feelings. At that time you will hardly need to remember how hard you worked and the words you relied on to comfort you. It is the structure they created within the brain that matters—a trained association between Upset and Calm Down, and among fear and calm and comfort. This automatic process is a chemical reaction that is guaranteed to bring relief and free up your confidence.

To begin this process, choose your words carefully, and use them until they are permanently implanted in your brain. In structuring your emotions you must select a comfort phrase that you will eventually no longer need.

Noam Chomsky, the formidable linguist at MIT, claims that grammatical structure—the rules for combining words into sentences—is independent of meaning. He illustrated his point with a much quoted sentence, "Colorless green ideas sleep furiously." The sentence follows the rules of grammar, but it makes no sense because it violates what we know to be true. A thing cannot be colorless and have color (green) at the same time; ideas do not have color or lack it; ideas do not sleep; sleep may be restless but not furious.

Contrarian that I am, this sentence means something to me. (Sorry, Professor Chomsky.) This sentence awakens emotion in me. I remember the self-pity I used to feel while churning awake in bed in the dark, early hours of the morning, my mind dragging up small hurts and concerns that I overreacted to. I felt so powerless, and anger—the action emotion—kept me awake.

Just as words can stir up, they can calm down. So, string comforting words together, even if they seem nonsensical, and give meaning to them. Now is the time to write yourself a very important message.

You can carry it with you in your pocket or purse, wallet or backpack, until one day you will no longer need it. Make sure you use the same comforting words. Do not attempt to apply different words for different upsetting emotional events. I want you to become attached to these words, and they will in time attach themselves internally to comfort your upsetting feelings.

Use your comfort words if you have bad dreams. Dreams are large advertising boards you drive by on life's highways. They are telling you how you *feel*, telling you what your emotions are. A dream in which you are chased by a monster and your legs will hardly move is a flashing sign: "Fear, victim, self-pity. Please help." A common dream I share with many is an image of myself arriving to take some impossibly difficult final examination and staring terrified with a blank mind as the earnest students around me scribble away and I can remember nothing. The message is clear: "Fear, stupid and humiliated, shame. Please send calm and comfort."

A dream that jolts you awake, where someone, perhaps you, is committing violence does not mean that you are a closet sociopath or potential murderer. The dream has an emotional message only: "Rage, revenge for humiliation (shame), or victimization (self-pity). Please calm down. Recognize the anger, and plan to act on it maturely and without blame."

These billboards are set up in your brain and flash on four to six times a night during REM sleep. These periods last on average fifteen to thirty minutes. Robert Stickgold and Allan Hobson, directors of Harvard University's neurophysiology lab and brilliant dream researchers, contend that "before a dream has a plot, characters, or setting, it gets assigned an emotion."

Use your dreams to uncover at night what you have felt during the day. I like to comfort myself and rewrite the sad and frightening ones. I tell myself, "Don't overreact." And then I like to give them happy, confident endings in which I am the brave heroine who slays whatever dragon was hurting me. Don't try to interpret your dreams, but use them as signposts of your emotional habits. Respond with a help line of comfort.

Repetition, repetition, rehearsal, rehearsal—learn your comfort phrase and repeat it over and over.

My own repeated struggle is to truly try to understand and help client after client, day after day. Experience comes from experience. For I have spent much of my adult life as a full-time, nine-to-six-every-day shrink, seeing one client after another and leading therapy groups. The experience of comfort is what you need, and only then can your natural-born confidence emerge.

Confidence: Finger Five. Finger Five is the thumb. The other four fingers point to the thumb. The thumb is holding the pencil I write with. Our sturdy thumb is the most vital and useful finger of all. Life would be much harder if we had to live without it—we would literally lose our grip. We handicap our confidence when emotional ties to the past weaken our grip on new opportunities. The opportunity to live life pain-free most of the time is surely not to be missed. All confident people have energy and they live by believing that anything is within their capability—for we do not strive for the ridiculous or insurmountable. I know that many who play life's game do not even think of future opportunities; they consider daily life to be enough, or even too much, of an ordeal. They will not know what they could have done.

Some years ago on a brilliant Florida morning, Noel, an Irish friend of mine, sat next to me in a deck chair on the seafront. We admired the elegant elderly folks who had gathered at Palm Beach's lovely Breakers Hotel for a hearty brunch and a good time. Noel and I were in our early thirties. He looked around the lovely scene, and suddenly turned serious, "Promise me, Sheenah, that we will not sit here, sunning ourselves, when we are old, having failed to achieve everything that is possible." This simple statement was as stunning to me as the beautiful ocean. I looked at the horizon and promised that I would not fail myself.

I want you to join me in that promise, no matter how you feel, despite your age, weight, and state of health, and despite your losing habits. Remember, emotional decisions are always a bad idea. I believe that most people, yes, even those who seem successful, are under-achievers. Lacking confidence, they make life difficult for themselves and fail to contribute all that they might. For confidence, unlike self-esteem, is not a hedonistic pursuit designed to enhance your personal image so you can beat out the rest. Confidence means utilizing one's natural brilliance and inherent confidence to give back to the world. When we die, this should be our influence and our legacy.

THE VALUE OF PERSISTENCE

When I explained the Winning Hand of Comfort to my client Sarah, she interrupted me, which is what people do when they fear hearing what I have to say. "This is harder than impossible," she interjected.

Take note of her predictions. Having grown up in a depressed fam-ily, Sarah was so set in her familiar self-pitying feelings that she angrily discounted my suggestion that there was much she could do to change. Can you guess what Sarah did when her painful feelings rose above the level she had grown so used to? She binged in a desperate attempt to calm down and return to the emotional level that felt normal for a while. Then she was miserable once more in her self-pity and shame.

When she managed to lose some weight and began feeling a little more attractive and sexy, she would soon binge again. Sarah was so ac-customed to feeling sad, sorry for herself, and angry that she would unconsciously undermine her own efforts and actively resist the help of all of her former therapists when they tried to intervene. Previous therapists who had told her that she could feel better threatened her sense of emotional security. Even though she wanted to ditch her de-pression, she did not feel that this was possible.

Now it was my turn. I knew that Sarah genuinely wanted to con-trol her feelings, and especially stop bingeing. She wanted to shoo away the critical vultures that circled in her brain. I recognized that her good intentions were at the mercy of those vultures—her own feelings. "It is hopeless," they would cry. "Accept that you are just a loser and always will be." These grotesque birds of her imagination pecked at her continually.

SARAH: I want to stop feeling like a fat loser. I really do.

SHEENAH: I know you do, but you keep telling me that my brain retraining prescription will never free you from your habitual self-criticism and helpless feelings.

SARAH: Look, I've tried for years. There have been countless fresh starts. I've spent a fortune on different kinds of therapy, and let's not forget the weight-loss stuff and the nutritionist. I am no better, just poorer.

SHEENAH: Sarah, you always bristle with anger when I do not sympathize with your helplessness. You sound as if there is a wheelchair in your brain that you can't imagine getting out of. I will not push you, but I know you can. You could start exercising your brilliant brain every day. In time you will be able to calm down and succeed in gaining the emotional stability you came to me for. But you have to do the work.

It is not unlikely that, like Sarah, you will interrupt me and tell me that you can't comfort yourself. Your feelings have a life of their own. It is not unlikely that you will fail to practice, like a child who finds piano lessons tedious and the technique hard to perfect. I cannot push you, but I can encourage and reassure you. Let me try:

- It is truly self-defeating to say that you are different, and that the Winning Hand of Comfort will not work for *you*.

- Humans learn by rehearsal. Those who practice find the task hard at first, but they soon improve.
- Given that all human beings are brilliant, you are equipped to succeed if you will persist.
- Persistence is exactly why you signed our Commitment Contract. Self-respect is only possible when you keep the promises you make to yourself.

Finally, let me remind you of the destructive confidence-zapping loser habits that will no longer be a source of *false* comfort, once you master the freedom prescription. For bingeing, pleasing, whining, procrastinating, and avoiding are immediate, unthought-out attempts to comfort feelings that have short-term appeal and painful long-term consequences.

When angry, upset, hurt, and humiliated, so many people make their situations worse. In fact, their attempts to calm their feelings make them more painful. The more upset they become, the farther they move away from fact and reason. Let me list some additional losing habits I have observed my clients slipping into when troubling feelings limit their lives. All of these attempts *fail* to comfort what T. S. Eliot called those "undisciplined squads of emotion."

- Raging and blaming—laying blame on others or on circumstances in order not to feel self-critical shame inside. Others will respond angrily.
- Obsessive worrying—the belief that worrying ahead of time can prevent bad things from happening. This is black magic, not preventative medicine. Worry promotes more things to worry about.
- Telling self-pitying stories about your miserable life in the hope of getting others to sympathize and comfort. Others will soon get annoyed.

- Inducing guilt in others with "you are lucky—it's all right for you" one-sided comparisons. Guilt is the service industry of the emotions business: "Take care of me, or you are mean, heartless, and uncaring." Guilt may invite attention at first, but soon others will feel exploited and avoid these attempts.

- Fantasies. Powerless children use fantasies to escape from situations they cannot change. Think how you fantasized when you were bored in school. Believing that it is better to dream than to deal with reality is a losing policy for adults, who can achieve nothing in their invented worlds.

- Magic. These emotional cures include depending on fortunetellers and gurus, waiting for the stars to get back into alignment, untested herbal remedies, and modern snake oils such as diet pills. All will fail and none will comfort feelings.

- Depression. When I hear the excuse "I'm depressed—I can't," I hear an opinion, not a fact. "I believe the future is hopeless, so I won't bother. I'm a loser." Even if you belong to the small group of people who meet the criteria for major depression and a skilled diagnostician has confirmed your diagnosis, you still need to assist your treatment by actively working with the Winning Hand of Comfort. No drug can deliver confidence or cause permanent positive change.

- Illnesses that are difficult to diagnose are mostly physical responses to an overstressed brain. Your body is complaining about the stress you are placing on your brain, and your immune system is less able to fight off infection and irritation.

- Compulsive orderliness. Seeking external order as a comfort policy makes a person a victim of a trivial time-consuming habit. It is impossible to live a germ-free life. No amount of cleaning and disinfecting will kill off these invisible companions. For people who rely on task completion for comfort, their "to do" list will outrun their energy. The list always wins.

Many of the false comfort habits listed above are to a degree understandable in small children. Adults who lack confidence also have a child trapped inside them, demanding to be free to discover a competent, brilliant self.

Let's be frank: You do not rent your body; you own it. You live there alone, so clean it, feed it, decorate it and, most of all, comfort it. It will then increase in value.

Let's be clear: Comforting your feelings allows the sun to rise in your brain. Only then can you see the horizon.

There is no time to waste. So, start now. Deal yourself the Winning Hand and play.

RX FREEDOM: THE PRESCRIPTION FOR CONFIDENCE

Take this prescription when you feel upset. Use it also when you are not upset. Its benefits increase with practice.

Calm *down a little.*

Clarify *the deeper feelings of shame and self-pity that lie beneath anger and anxiety.*

Challenge *vigorously the thinking and behavior that generate these feelings, and then apply the salve of*

Comfort—*i.e., your own personal words. Repeat your comfort phrase, and the result will be*

Confidence—*the freedom to react calmly and effectively to real difficulties, and to be free of painful feelings.*

EIGHT

THE PROBLEM WITH ANGER: BULLIES AND VICTIMS

A tiny green iguana scuttered across a sandy path, startling a young woman in a bikini. She was strolling to the beach on a beautiful Caribbean island, relishing the fact that a winter blizzard was raging in her hometown. In the shade of the palm trees that lined her path it was 75 degrees.

"What a sweet baby he is," she said as she turned to search for the iguana. Failing to notice a rock in the path, she tripped. She fell forward, cutting her toe and grazing her hands as she tried to save herself. "You stupid, stupid idiot," she shouted out loud to the empty air. Ruefully rubbing her wounds, she had a flash of insight. "Why am I so quick to anger and blame myself all the time?" She thought about her boyfriend, who had recently dumped her, telling her that he loved her but not her temper. She would angrily blame him, too, when things were not to her liking. This vacation was her attempt to heal her broken heart. She knew that her angry attitude at work was hampering her chances for promotion. "My confidence is at an all-time low," she wept. "How is it that I am kinder to a small lizard than I am to myself?" she asked.

Let's be frank: Venting anger is not good for you or your confidence.

Let's be clear: Confident people don't vent. They take effective action.

They take the effective action of reducing or eliminating frustration. It is frustration that sparks anger, and the frustration can be actual, physical, or psychological, in the past, the present, or in a prediction of the future.

An *actual* loss of a relationship, property, or money can stir us to feel anger. *Physical* attacks of any kind by people, animals, germs, and viruses will always anger us. Fortunately, losses, both actual and physical, rarely occur.

Psychologically, we get angry when someone or something threatens to break our personal rules of living (the way we believe life ought to be). Our rules include our sense of justice, our value system, our moral code, our religious beliefs, and our political viewpoint. But do not be fooled into thinking that anger is a well-reasoned, logical response. Many of our rules are irrational and some are just plain nutty.

Most of the anger you and I experience has a psychological base. People who lack confidence are so self-critical and feel so vulnerable and sensitive that only a thin membrane of self-respect stands between them and the world. When criticized, ignored, excluded, unapplauded, or overlooked, they erupt into anger, either losing their temper or sulking and withdrawing.

An emotional habit is not only based on past experiences. Memories of those events will continue to shape how we view ourselves and the world. To illustrate this point simply, children, familiar with onslaughts of rage and humiliation, will as adults continue to see the world as a critical, hostile place. They unconsciously create a cycle of anger. Timid and fearful, they imagine criticism and believe they hear it in people's remarks, even when this is not true. They try to fend off conflict by complying, and attempt to please the authority figures they fear. Chronically anxious, they are usually angry with themselves for what they see as their own weakness and inadequacy. Their emotionally overloaded brains easily slip into depression. Many will binge in a bid to find relief from their feelings, and then angrily blame themselves for their defeating habit.

Alternatively, children raised by indulgent parents without sufficient rules or discipline (a parenting policy that seems prevalent in the U.S.A. at this point in history) view the world as a resource to satisfy their desires. Irresponsible and self-indulgent, they angrily resent restrictions and are overly sensitive to criticism, normal setbacks, and disappointments. They react with rage when thwarted, and are quick to be irritable and to feel sorry for themselves. Disliking limits, they too are prone to binges and addictions.

Let's be frank: To criticize and blame oneself breeds shame and anger.

Let's be clear: To criticize and blame others and the world spawns self-pity and anger.

Shame and self-pity, the moralizing emotions, are the bedrock from which anger erupts. People who are touchy, thin-skinned, and oh-so-sensitive are both the bullies *and* the victims. Fearful of victimization or humiliation, they will overreact by raging or sulking whenever they perceive that an insult has occurred. Their immature anger habits undermine their confidence and the confidence of those around them. Criticism, unhappiness, and especially anger are as contagious as the common cold.

THE MOTIVATION BEHIND BLAME

I once counseled a man whose wife wanted to divorce him. "It's my fault," he lamented. "I'm just stupid. I don't pay enough attention to my wife. I work too much, and"—he hesitated—"I can never satisfy her sexually. I'm a bit shy in bed. I've put on some weight and she hates that. No wonder she wants to leave me. I'm just a loser."

I met separately with his wife, who said: "He's a lousy husband, inattentive, a workaholic, and just not attractive any more. He put on over twenty-five pounds in the last few years and he's out of shape. He is so weak and a lousy lover. He *is* a good provider, but that's not enough for me."

The man was very critical of himself. He deprived himself of confidence with his beliefs that he was stupid, fat, and a loser in bed and in marriage. His wife was very critical of him, and helped him to undermine his confidence with her angry nagging. What do you think they have in common?

The answer is *blame*. She felt sorry for herself, and blamed him for the deprivation she felt in her marriage. He blamed himself, and felt ashamed and angry about his "inadequacies." They both, as I later discovered, blamed themselves for staying in a miserable marriage, and blamed each other for being weak and unmanly, or bossy and critical. He avoided open conflict, and although he seemed to accept her disrespectful accusations, he stewed with inner wrath. She blamed herself for being so nasty and treating him so badly. Each day she would strive to be pleasant but, feeling deprived of companionship, sex, and connection, she would allow a wellspring of self-pity to spew forth in a tirade of invective. Everything about him seemed to irritate her.

I insisted they stop blaming, at least while in my presence. I explained that blaming others for our plight is a clear defense against the shame we might feel were we to look at our part in the problem. On the other hand, to blame oneself entirely overlooks the contributions the other person makes to a situation, self-centeredly focusing on those critical shame ideas you now know well on the fingers of the Losing Hand: Stupid, Fat, Old, Ugly, and Loser.

I decided to see this couple separately, and work with their individual emotional habits. The husband recognized his self-critical shame habit, and was relieved when I persuaded him to stop seeing himself as the sole cause of his wife's unhappiness. He enjoyed learning to stand his ground, especially his new policy of insisting that she stop criticizing him. He was intrigued to discover that this not only worked, but that it did not cause a fight if he insisted without criticizing her.

The wife was quite reluctant to stop criticizing him, at first. I had to work hard to get her to stop interrupting *me* when I tried to stop her complaining. "But you don't understand," she repeatedly said, "he does this or he doesn't do that." I pointed out that her list of dissatisfactions were of little importance, and that her harsh judgments did not encourage him to cooperate with her.

The turning point came when she told me how much she disliked herself for her angry, bullying ways. They began to communicate honestly and without blame. The commonalities that had brought them together reemerged from beneath a fog of anger. Neither really wanted a divorce, but both used the threat of a divorce to punish the other. Never ask for an exit visa, unless you really mean it, was my request to them. The mention of divorce faded away as their marriage bloomed again.

Let's be frank: Confident people are not bullies. They do not angrily blame others.

Let's be clear: Confident people are not victims. They do not act like immature children, crying, complaining, and labeling themselves as "bad" when normal reversals occur.

THE MANAGEMENT OF ANGER

The noted theorist and researcher into the nature of emotions Robert Plutchik sums up the positive and negative aspects of anger. As he wrote in his article, "The Nature of Emotion," in *The American Scientist*, "Anger intimidates, influences others to do something you wish them to do, energizes an individual for attack or defense and spaces the participants in a conflict."

This chapter is designed to show you how to train your brain to manage angry feelings in a calm, confident, and therefore mature manner. Anger, as you are no doubt aware, can be a very dangerous emotion to act upon. Anger should be a signal only—a sign that there is a problem to deal with. *A feeling of anger is not a permit to express it.*

Now, let me challenge you to a quiz. When faced with insult, betrayal, disappointment, humiliation, victimization or loss, which of the following is the confident response?

1. Get angry, blame, and try to seek revenge.
2. Guilt-trip the person who is to blame into submission.
3. Sulk in order to invite sympathy and persuade the person who has hurt you to feel guilty, apologize, and acquiesce.
4. Avoid potential conflict by accepting the blame, even if you are not responsible.
5. Complain in private but keep quiet to avoid making the situation worse.
6. Calm down, think carefully, and decide on the best strategy to deal with the problem.

I expect you chose number 6. If number 6 is your normal, everyday response to the real (and not imagined) challenges you face, you are one of the confident few who play with a Winning Hand. You do not trust your feelings or make emotional decisions. As the quiz demonstrates, we often know what is the right way to act when angered, but do not listen to our own rules of mature behavior and instead we act directly on our feelings.

THE WHY OF IT

If we know the right way to act, why would any of us ever disregard our own wise advice? Why overreact angrily—raging, sulking, complaining, blaming, demanding, avoiding, and hiding out? Why do we act on feelings of anger and anxiety rather than calming down and using our high-level, thinking brain to figure out a wise response? Why do we show *a lack of confidence* in our problem-solving, conflict-resolving ability by wasting energy venting anger? We complain, "It is unfair—why can't people see my point of view and do things right?" But they don't. Does this stop us? No. We just get angrier and try to preach to them, or find subtle ways to punish them into submission, or seek revenge—and damage our relationships.

Later, many of us will feel ashamed, guilty, and remorseful. These feelings further undermine our own confidence, a sour dessert to the entrée of a just-burned relationship. The appetizer—the dumb event that set us off—seems so unimportant now—at least until the next time.

Rather than overreacting and beating ourselves up, it would make more sense to learn from our mistakes so that the next time will be different. I much prefer to call mistakes "experiments," "research," or "dry runs." So-called mistakes should be seen as efforts to find solutions, as failures can promote new ideas and eventually more successful results. Advances in science are made this way. And when we bake or learn to drive we improve after making mistakes and we grow in confidence with increasing competence.

So why is it different with anger and other emotional habits? Why do we react with the same familiar, troublemaking, misery-causing angry episodes that, despite our apologies and new resolutions, we just repeat? The answer lies in our pasts. In his book *The Blank Slate: The Modern Denial of Human Nature*, Stephen Pinker presents research evidence from many studies. These studies show that all people, no matter how different their cultures, have the same set of emotional expressions. The capacity to feel anger, like other emotions, is in our genes. How we manage anger comes from our upbringing. We learn what our family considers to be the proper way to show annoyance. I hear stories from clients about how shocked they felt when visiting a friend whose family had a different anger style. "Can you believe it?" a teenager asked me. "My friend and her parents screamed insults at each other, then we all sat down and enjoyed a happy dinner together. If I had raised my voice and spoken to my parents that way I would have been grounded for a year."

We live in reaction to our parents, but we also learn what works and what doesn't work, and how we do not want to act and be. I knew when I was a young college student that I had a problem with anger. I would be bad-tempered, irritable, and even nasty at home, yet passive, nervous, and pleasing to others at school. I constantly promised myself that I would be kinder to my mother and stop acting like a grizzly bear like my father, and I resolved to speak up if my teachers' feedback annoyed me. I soon broke my promises, and then I would feel even more angry and ashamed. I am such a loser, I thought, poking even more holes in the thin veil of confidence I possessed at the time. I just could not control my emotional responses. I wanted to reform, but I would soon relapse into my own old familiar passive ways.

Have you ever mixed a martini? It is all a matter of personal preference as to what the ingredients are—a measure of an individually selected gin or vodka—not too much or too little. A flavoring of white, dry vermouth—a trickle or a mere drop, according to taste. Add some ice, stir, and pour into a proper martini glass. We pop in an olive or a tiny onion or maybe a twist of lemon. The cocktail could also be served plain. Others' taste may seem unfamiliar to you, but for a martini enthusiast the flavor must always be the same and the mix familiar. It is a precise science.

And so it is with anger styles. A complex cocktail of personal angry reactions is present in every adult, ready to be stirred up when hurt, damage, and deprivation to our person, our property, or our self-respect occur. It is important to mention here that these events often evoke fear that mixes with our anger, confusing us by creating indecision. (In chapter 9 we will take on and overcome the habits of fear and anxiety that erode confidence.)

At birth it is not so complex. Anger is about survival. Wet, hungry, scared, needy, we cry out angrily for aid and assistance. By the time we reach adulthood the way we express anger has become far more individual and complex. We all feel anger, even those who do not realize it (or claim not to). Our angry reactions have a precise format blended from a mix of responses we learned and practiced as we grew up.

Thus we have individually formulated an anger style that we return to every time we get angry. An anger habit is established that is so familiar that we just react without thinking about the effect on ourselves or the impact on others.

In a sense, nature supplied the engine, but our family unwittingly provides the spark plugs and ignition. Some people's anger engines are always idling, ready to accelerate to top speed whenever there is an upset. Others' anger engines are slow to start, but spark up with frightening speed when the pressure builds and builds to a breaking point. Some never seem to start, but the buildup of internal combustion eventually causes structural problems—in human terms, stress-induced depression and physical illnesses.

The problem is that the familiar is tempting. As a naturalized American, born and raised in Britain, I still prefer fish and chips and tea to pizza and beer, and I even like gray, rainy days. Familiar tastes and smells make me feel at home and give me a sense of security, a reminder that I know who I am and where I come from. Sadly for me, my familiar and secure way of expressing anger was immature and destructive, both to my relationships and to my sense of self-respect. "You are such a baby," my friends told me. In regard to my anger habit they were right. I was continually damaging my confidence.

Let's be frank: Shame and self-pity are the bases of immature anger.

Let's be clear: Immature anger keeps us "trapped like a trap in a trap," to quote Dorothy Parker.

Take a long hard look at the Losing Hand in Anger. Pay particular attention to Fingers One, Two, and Three. (See following page.)

These three fingers describe the anger style of those of us who react in emotionally immature ways. When we are mad, like small chil-

Losing Hand in Anger

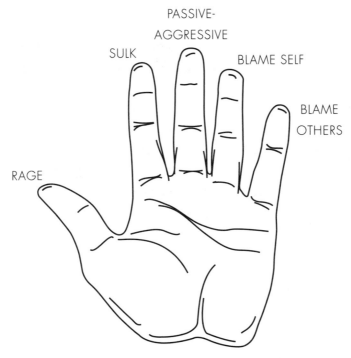

RAGE: Attempts to humiliate with insults. Threatens to abandon. Falsely expresses dislike and even hatred for victims.

SULK: Internally held rage. Refusal to communicate for prolonged periods. Refusal to be comforted or apologized to. Impatient and overly sensitive to criticism.

PASSIVE-AGGRESSIVE: Indirectly expresses anger. Induces guilt in others. Arrives late, is forgetful and unreliable. Avoids sex and affection. Humiliates with humor and/or in public. Opposes others' wishes.

BLAME SELF: Passive responses to any criticism or accusation. "It must be my fault." Apologizes even when not in the wrong. Avoids criticism. Exquisitely sensitive to criticism, except from self.

BLAME OTHERS: Whines and complains, attributing problems to others' stupidity. Labels others with insulting names. Sees world as threatening. Predicts future trouble. Irritable, untrusting, jealous. Does not apologize.

dren, we rage, sulk, or attempt to make others feel guilty. We hope that those upsetting us will relent, apologize, and solve our problems for us. This wish undermines confidence, as it actually invites others to avoid us or rebel against us. Thus we make ourselves madder, becoming increasingly accusatory and irrational, as all those who rage and sulk do. Eventually, we give up and feel embarrassed and ashamed of our behavior, promising ourselves that we won't overreact again. But habits are powerful, familiar, and attractive. We fall back into them every time.

A client of mine described herself as an "angry Chihuahua." Used to feeling sorry for herself, she could find pseudoreasons to feel badly treated in every facet of her life. She collected a grudge library—memories of small slights and misperceptions to support her self-pity habit. Exquisitely sensitive to disagreement, criticism, or others' discontent, she angered easily, creating a volume of rage that would explode into a tirade of furious yapping. She hated the tiny yapper inside her, but also felt protected by giving vent to it. She was all feeling. She took no time to think about the validity of her perceptions or the severity of the many infractions she daily felt disrespected by. There was no room for empathy—she was too furious to think clearly about what others might be feeling and what their intentions really were, and how she might respond more powerfully.

It was a joyful experience for both of us to help her come to terms with her blaming, bullying rage. We strove to understand its origins in her critical, quarrelsome family, and to stop her loud insistence that she was right and others stupid. What emerged from under this cloud of self-pity and hostility that caused others to fear and dislike her was a good-humored, fun-loving person who, with confidence, developed an external blame-free way of asking for respect and an internal comforting habit that brought her peace. The dog is dead. Long live the lady!

Adults must resolve conflict themselves in effective ways that are both respectful and influential to others. Raging, sulking, and passive-aggressiveness in adults invite opposition and disrespect, not conflict resolution. Recognize your anger as a signal—and only a signal—that something is wrong. Refusing to act on this feeling, a mature person in conflict calms down a little and figures out a proper response.

DO YOU HAVE AN IMMATURE ANGER STYLE?

Do you know if you have an immature anger style? Fingers One, Two, and Three may clearly describe you, but if you are still confused, look at the clues in the Immature Anger Style Checklist that follows. Each of the following statements represents an immature style of anger. Do one or more of them apply to you and other people you know?

Finger One: Rage

- Easily loses temper.

Finger Two: Sulk

- Falls silent and sulks
- Cries and tries to inspire guilt and gain sympathy from others when mad
- Withdraws, stews, and obsesses about slights and rejection

Finger Three: Passive-aggressive expressions

- Complains of unfairness and criticizes others behind their backs
- Agrees, concedes, and even apologizes to avoid conflict, but then anger builds up and eventually explodes into an irrational rage
- Uses sarcasm or an insulting sense of humor to punish others
- Opposes passively, such as avoiding situations, being late or uncooperative
- Criticizes and demeans someone in the presence of others so he or she can't easily retaliate.

Finger Four: Blame of self—shame

- Feels guilty when others are angry
- Gets angry and blames self when things go wrong
- Depressed—feels powerless, unhappy, and hopeless (also Finger Five)
- Makes negative predictions about the future

Finger Five: Blame of others—self-pity

- Gets angry and blames others, insisting on own innocence
- Gets angry with family members whenever they are upset or angry
- Is impatient and easily bored
- Highly sensitive to criticism—thin-skinned, unstable, and moody
- Depressed—feels powerless and hopeless about the possibility of change

If your answer is yes to any these statements, you have a good idea as to what you will need to change. Begin now by not blaming yourself for this discovery (Finger Four), and not blaming your family, either (Finger Five). You will learn how to take charge of your anger in this chapter, and never forget that blaming yourself creates shame, while blaming others generates self-pity.

Let me remind you how feelings of shame and self-pity damage motivation and extinguish hope. If you were sitting on my couch, you, like many of my clients, would likely ask the following questions, for change can be threatening. Moving on, leaving home, and saying good-bye to our old familiar ways should only be undertaken for very sound reasons. The reason I offer you an invitation to change the anger habits that undermine your confidence is that they invite others to treat you disrespectfully and act angrily toward you. Let me try to persuade you by addressing your queries.

Ragers often justify their habits by asking me to agree with two basic assumptions. "But Sheenah, surely it is human nature to express feelings in a raw fashion."

No, I explain, it is certainly human to *have* feelings. Only small children need to express loud anger in order to make a large impact. Bullies may feel powerful, but they are never confident. They cannot stand criticism and threaten those who dare. No one respects bullies. Compliance to a bully's wishes through fear will lead to eventual rebellion. Bullies often lose husbands, wives, jobs, employees, and the support of neighbors. Yet many are loath to risk changing their old ways. They fear being shamed. So they want to humiliate others first.

"Okay, Sheenah, but surely it is healthy to vent feelings. I feel better afterward and I don't keep my anger in and get depressed."

No, I reply, it is *un*healthy to vent. Venting ignores others' feelings. If you bully people with your feelings by blaming them, they may cooperate through fear, but will certainly get back at you later. Others who are not intimidated will fight you, a struggle that goes nowhere, as people get more irrational and self-righteous the angrier they get.

But wait, there's more. Venting does not actually make you feel better. We certainly should be aware of our feelings and express them appropriately, but "venting" is not an effective way to prevent illness or depression. So, be wary of those who advise punching pillows or having a good scream as a health-giving activity. Adults are not steam engines that need to let out steam to relieve pressure. In fact, to express anger loudly and in an accusatory tone over a long period of time helps rage to build. Angry exaggeration drives more and more temper. Brad Bushman, a psychologist at Iowa State University, studied the "catharsis hypothesis"—the proposition that expressing anger expels it and calms a person down. His subjects got angry as they beat on a punching bag; later in the day they were observed to behave far *more* aggressively toward others than usual, not *less* aggressively.

"But Sheenah, it's hard for me to calm down when I am mad. If I take a walk, work out, meditate, or do some yoga, I feel calmer. I read in the newspapers that exercise calms the brain." Yes, I know that temporary relief from stressful anger can be achieved through exercise and the like, but most of the time when upset occurs we just can't run to the gym or take time out. These tactics can provide a little bit of calm, but they are no substitute for the mature practice of calming oneself when angry. Exercise your lungs if you struggle with this first step in the Winning Hand of Comfort; slowing our breathing slows us down emotionally, just a little and just enough to get on with the remaining steps.

Here are some of the usual questions people ask whose anger style is best described by Fingers Two and Three (sulking and passive-aggressive expressions): "But Sheenah, I hate anger. I get upset and withdraw. If only people would leave me alone and give me my space, I get over it. I am not a bully."

I disagree! Sulkers are *quiet* bullies. To take time off from a relationship is self-centered. I mean that. It takes no account of how the other person feels or the likelihood that they will feel punished by your withdrawal and get angry. So, as a conflict-avoiding policy, sulking and passive-aggressive punishment—subtle bullying—invite hostility.

"But Sheenah, are you telling me I should not complain when others do not treat me fairly? I believe that crying just shows how upset I am. Why should I hide my feelings?" My answer: Like venting anger, crying and complaining make you feel more helpless and sorry for yourself. They are in fact bullying tactics and essentially immature. By acting as a victim you attempt to make others feel guilty in hopes of getting them to comply and comfort you. Complainers soon annoy those around them, and crying increases helpless self-pity and self-righteous anger. If you are a crier, do not believe that this habit is inborn (genetic) or simply the response of a very sensitive person. Crying is very influential and can contain a lot of anger. It is hard to let a baby cry for long, and so it is with adults. Unless we comfort them, we will feel guilt and shame and, eventually, anger. So, do not overlook the bullying aspect of tears.

I hope I have convinced you that in the interests of confidence you must revolutionize your anger style now that you understand your familiar pattern.

As you know, people love familiarity and the abiding sense of comfort it provides, and find it tough to venture into new and unfamiliar emotional territory. But there is a pioneer in all of us—an adventurer who seeks new experiences. The desire to develop and mature is genetic, too. In our own way, we are all revolutionaries who plan to change ourselves for the better. Why else would you be reading this book?

The city of Birmingham, where I was born and raised, lies at the center of the gritty West Midlands in England. In more bucolic times this area produced William Shakespeare. It is here in the late eighteenth century that the first metal chains were forged to replace the thick hemp ropes that were used to tether the great ships of a seafaring nation. This simple-sounding breakthrough changed the world, for the Industrial Revolution was as much a seismic shift as the electronic technology movement is today. The West Midlands area itself is one of sudden shifts, from the green hedges and tidy villages of the English postcard countryside to the decaying factories and mean streets of grim row houses divided by dismal alleyways.

This area has produced its share of rebels. Every year on the night of November 5th, children burn effigies of Guy Fawkes, the Osama bin Laden of his time; at the last minute, his angry plot to blow up both the king and the Houses of Parliament with several wooden barrels of gunpowder hidden in the basement was foiled. In the industrial suburbs of Birmingham, the rebellious leader of the group Black Sabbath forged the heavy-metal music that shocked a generation of parents. Later, when he had become a world-famous rock-and-roll star but still a rebel, Ozzy Osbourne declared, in his usual poetic manner, that a person who cannot stand his ground is as useless as "a one-legged man in an ass-kicking contest."

I want the impact of *Complete Confidence* to rock you and cause you to shift by revolutionizing the way you manage and express anger.

Do you regard the feeling of anger only as a warning signal? Do you calm yourself and think carefully about how to deal with what threatens you? Do you then powerfully and calmly work toward resolving conflict in a respectful manner? Do you speak out honestly and without blame when dissatisfied or hurt? Do you calmly and without blame insist on respect when genuinely insulted? Is yours the voice of reason when others are making emotional decisions?

If not, you are undermining your confidence and we must rebel against this.

WHY FIGHT?

I find that most of my clients have a utopian wish for a world I call Planet Pleasant. In this world there is no anger (or not much), no criticism, no unkindness, no jealousy, no envy, no battles, and no war. The dry seeds of the "Make Love Not War" sixties are still blowing in the wind. Unskilled at managing anger, its proponents would choose to eliminate it, if such magic were possible.

But I stand in defense of anger, the tough emotion that provides the shield and sword we need when physically or emotionally assaulted. Avoidance is Finger Five on the second Losing Hand, and is a contributor to a lack of confidence. So, we need to set forth a workable proposal that deals not only with modifying your anger style, but also with its foundation of buried and often unrecognized feelings that cause anger to bubble up.

For anger is in the air. We hear it, we feel it every day, often many times over. Anger floats in the space around us: We overhear a couple fighting in the hotel room next door; raised voices across a crowded parking lot; an irritable mother chiding her small children. Anger is not toxic, and we can never expect to be free of it.

Internally, irritation stirs us up. Anger and anxiety are fast-acting. When we detect a threat, signals race to the amygdala, a small part of the limbic system deep inside the brain—Emotion Central. Shame, guilt, and self-pity seem to come on more slowly and are longer-lasting and pervasive. These chronic, slow-moving, plodding emotions can haunt us for long periods. Anger arrives fast like the hare; shame and self-pity relentlessly trudge like the tortoise.

We are all more aware of anger than these other feelings, and I shall prove it. When I decided to make a list of all the anger words and phrases I could muster, I was surprised at how many words there are to describe angry people. Here are some of them. Let me know if you have others (I am a collector): bully, nasty, touchy, thin-skinned, bratty, a baby, a curmudgeon, a nightmare, a monster, Godzilla, "she's on the rag" (a phrase to make women see red), a bitch, an iron lady, pissy, and (lately) a terrorist. *Roget's Thesaurus* has over twenty words to describe anger. The ones I like are the most unusual: wrath, ire, and vexation.

On the other hand, there is a noticeable paucity of words in regular usage to describe a person with a shame habit. The same is true for self-pity. I used "whiner" in the second Losing Hand, and people can be labeled "complainers." I couldn't find more than those in any of my dictionaries. Shame is hardly recognized and self-pity is avoided. People do not readily describe themselves as self-pitiers; they would feel too much shame if they were to acknowledge this helpless feeling, and so they avoid the label.

What interests me even more are the warning phrases well-meaning people use to alert others to potential anger that is more subtle and punitive in nature: the sudden rare rages of the passive bully or the punishing withdrawal of the passive-aggressive. Here are some of their wise warnings:

Don't get on her wrong side.
He has a chip on his shoulder.
She has an ax to grind.
Don't be fooled by his Mr. Nice Guy act.
Don't trust her—what you see is not *what you get.*

He is a pain in the ass.

She has a stick up her ass. (Both of these painful scenarios would
    make us all angry.)

Wait until you get the silent treatment.

She loses it.

Watch your back with him.

She is likely to have a hissy fit.

So many of us are regularly angry or in an angry mood, like rebels without much of a cause. We overuse our anger—the valuable, protective emotion—and do not reserve it for its true purpose.

For how many genuine threats to life and limb and property have you faced this week? I hope—and know for most of us—the answer is zero. Sadly, as we progress through life, all of us will very rarely but certainly face serious threats and will respond with a combination of fear and anger. Anger might just empower us enough to overcome an attacker if necessary. Yet, most events we react to angrily are psychological—what some people like to call damage to the ego or pride. Anger should be a signal only—to get busy and rationally figure out a potentially winning strategy for the trouble we face.

So, why do we fail to act rationally? Why do we get angry about others' minute actions or inactions? Why are we whiny and bossy, irritable and irritating, critical and catty, sulky and sarcastic, and so easily pissed off? And what prevents us from starting a peace movement within ourselves in order to live outside of our negative, critical, angry feelings and experience the world calmly and positively most of the time? This surely beats living in our heads, mulling over today's "insult" or tomorrow's potential victimization.

The answer to the question "why?" is in your own losing hands (Fingers Four and Five). Look again at the thinking habits of everyone who lacks confidence: the self-descriptions that mass produce shame and self-pity and much unnecessary anger.

The self-descriptions on the Losing Fingers are hot buttons—units

The Losing Hand 1

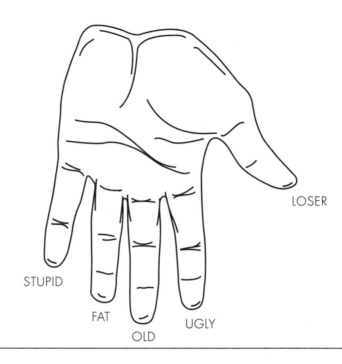

LOSER

STUPID

FAT

OLD   UGLY

of shame and self-pity that command attention every day. They burn internally, and if others touch these sore spots, even inadvertently, they hurt, rage rises, anger erupts, and irritation sets in.

When I feel stupid, I will overreact if you dare to imply that my self-perception is at all accurate. I will not tolerate any criticism. I will be quick to call *you* and your view of me "stupid" under my breath if I am childlike and fearful. Understand that "stupid" is *my* prerogative. Stay off my turf!

But wait, it gets worse. I don't even need *you* to criticize me. I can create shame and anger all by myself. I will unconsciously act in ways that make me feel stupid and invite you to agree with my critical view of myself. Look at the second Losing Hand.

The Losing Hand 2

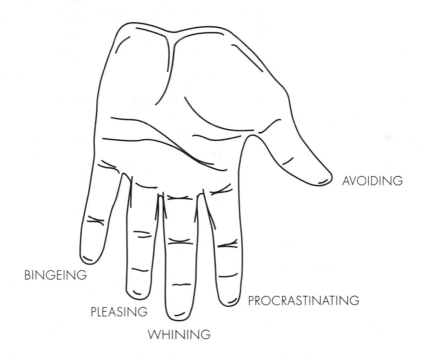

AVOIDING

BINGEING

PLEASING

PROCRASTINATING

WHINING

See how I binge despite my resolution not to. Watch me please you and agree with you and let you make the decisions because I'm scared you will be mad at me. Hear me whine and complain, weakly hoping you will comfort and reassure me. See how I procrastinate, avoiding the possibility of producing something stupid or fearful of being bored and, of course, sorry for myself. I don't act responsibly. Watch me avoid social and business opportunities, asking a guy for a date (he could reject me), going to parties alone (no one cares about me), missing out on sex (rejection fears again), and refusing to speak in public (you might think I'm a stupid idiot).

All of these behaviors are gilt-edged, emotionally expensive invitations to others to actually criticize you and eventually reject your company. Others might point out your neediness, your unreliability, your indecisiveness, and your complaining. Do you thank them for the insight? No, you will get mad—mad at yourself—and mad at them. For you unwittingly set them up to be the villain in your play; in it, you are the shame-filled, self-pitying victim and they are the bad guys.

Victims are always angry, yet continue to think, act, and feel sorry for themselves. Angry over and over again, day after day, year after year, self-pitiers repeatedly undermine confidence by handicapping themselves at work, in their relationships with others, and with themselves.

Let's be frank: A victim's self-pity leads to rage.

Let's be clear: Confident people don't think of themselves as victims.

For we are the problem—we make trouble for ourselves. We stick painful splinters into our own skin. So, every time you feel angry, before you make a move, review and revisit the Winning Hand of Comfort.

HOW TO CHANGE AN ANGER HABIT

I have already described the Winning Hand of Comfort in chapter 7. Here I will show you how to apply it specifically to anger.

Finger One: Calm. In some people, anger heats up fast and boils over; in others, it stews and simmers for a long time. Take the pot off the stove before you burn yourself and others, and have a mess to clean up. Slow your breathing. Stop and think. Try holding your forehead when you get angry or put your hands over your ears for a moment to give yourself the all-important nanosecond of calming. Angry reactions are about acting, not thinking first. Don't trust your feelings, and don't act on them. With just a little more calm, you can think better.

The Winning Hand of Comfort

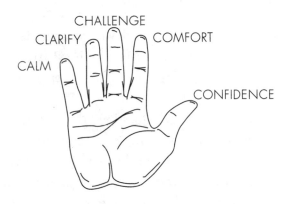

CHALLENGE
CLARIFY
COMFORT
CALM
CONFIDENCE

CALM
Calm yourself a bit by breathing slowly.
Tell yourself to calm down.
In seconds your brain will clear just enough for you to think.

CLARIFY
Clarify your thinking.
Ask: Am I angry? Go deeper. Ask: What am I feeling ashamed/ humiliated about? Now you can recognize your shame habit.
And/or ask: Am I feeling anxious? Go deeper. Ask: What am I feeling sorry for myself about? (Feeling helpless or hopeless)
Now you can recognize your self-pity habit.

CHALLENGE
Challenge your thinking.
Ask: What am I blaming myself for? (Creating shame)
Ask: What am I blaming others misfortune or the world for? (Creating self-pity)
Reframe your thoughts without blame. Write them down if this helps.

COMFORT
Comforting your feelings is the key to confidence.
Repeat over and over again your preferred words of comfort. Say the same words every time.
Write your comfort phrase here:

Do this until you physically feel the drug of Freedom begin to calm your brain, freeing it from high levels of anger and anxiety.
Never miss an opportunity to practice this until you have created an automatic comfort habit.

CONFIDENCE
You will think clearly, act wisely, and never make emotional decisions.
You will be free of reactive anger and anxiety, living in the world and not locked in an emotionally overloaded brain.
The drug of Freedom flows freely, coming automatically to your aid when you are upset.

Let's be frank: Unmanaged anger is far more of a problem than the action that precipitated it.

Let's be clear: Manage your feelings well and your life is well managed.

Finger Two: Clarify. Render down the angry feelings to their basic ingredients. What are your deeper feelings? Are you feeling shame? Self-pity? Are you insulting yourself or others with the fingers of the Losing Hand?

Finger Three: Challenge. Question all of the thoughts that lead to the shame and self-pity that jump-start your anger, and demand proof that they are true. Write them down and review your thinking with some objectivity. Expect them to be exaggerated or just plain false.

Let's be frank: We often justify our feelings with biased blaming and irrational thinking. Do not trust this thinking, either.

Let's be clear: Question and query your thoughts.

Finger Four: Comfort. Apply the comforting phrase that you created, when you have calmed a little and clarified your feelings. Eventually, through repetition, upset will automatically be associated with comforting words—putting you in control of your anger.

Some clients say, "I can handle it. It will be okay." A famous Yankee baseball player known for his unflappable attitude says to himself, "Everything's going to be all right."

Finger Five: Confidence—the last finger on the Winning Hand of Comfort. Confidence means that you are in control even when angered. When you are angry you can now decide to react in one of the three following ways.

Option One. If you have been truly disrespected, you can speak up without blame, in a calm, confident, mature tone. Don't say, "You hurt my feelings," unless you are under age fifteen. "Hurt feelings" signal weakness and an appeal for pity. Adults mostly hurt their own feelings. Instead say, "I feel disrespected by your statement (or action), but I am very unclear as to whether this is an accurate perception." Frame this response in your own words and in your own way, but promise to stop at the full stop and listen carefully to the other person with an open mind. Do not butt in and disagree. You are not a litigating attorney, or if you are, save your interruption for the courtroom.

Option Two. Say little or nothing and focus on calming and comforting yourself. Recognize the possibility that you imagined or created and are overreacting to an unfair act or situation, seeking an opportunity to regenerate the same old familiar anger response to your shame or self-pity habits. You are about to be a troublemaker, so do nothing but comfort yourself.

Option Three. Take your focus off how you feel and instead take the truly mature step of asking yourself, "What could this person, who acted in a way that caused me to feel anger, be thinking and feeling? It does not make sense. Let me think about it."

Let's be frank: When others act in ways that do not make sense to you the reason is psychological, not logical (right or wrong).

Let's be clear: Their psychological reaction is not necessarily about you.

Here are some examples:

A snappy wife is not "a misery or a bitch," but could be tired or premenstrual (a temporary biological state that exaggerates existing negative feelings).

A silent husband is not "self-centered or disinterested in his wife," but could be preoccupied with worries of his own (potential shame, self-pity, and anger).

A whiny teenager is not just "an ungrateful pain in the neck," but may possibly be feeling loser shame and anger.

An unappreciative, critical boss is not just "having a bad day," but could fear the loss of control of the business or the shame of being criticized herself.

A procrastinating employee is not just "lazy," but could fear the shame of feeling incompetent or the self-pity of his boss's censure.

In asking you to consider Option Three—what the offender might be thinking and feeling—I am suggesting you take a mature, empathic position, rather than overreacting with critical misjudgment and then rage or passive sulking. I'll explain this later in the chapter.

OPTION ONE IN ACTION

Let me remind you, anger is your signal, a red warning light. But it does not give you the green light to act on it. If after managing your anger you decide rationally and thoughtfully to take Option One, here are some examples of what to do and say.

Option One. Speak up without blame if truly disrespected, in a calm, confident manner.

Step 1. Use the first person singular—"I." "You" can be heard as accusatory. Make a *short* statement and shut up. The fewer words, the better. The more moderate the tone, the more powerful the delivery.

Give no justifications, no evidence of the other's wrongdoing, no insults, no swear words, no excuses, no apologies. Never say, "I am sorry to have to say this." Do not cry, do not plead, and never be dramatic or hysterical. Just simply make a statement. Repeat it once, word for word if necessary. In advertising and in political campaigns, influence is achieved by repeating the sound byte or message. Propaganda works—so repeat your message verbatim every time a person tries to bully you.

Here are some of my casebook samples:

Manager to assistant (in a loud voice): This report is a piece of garbage. What is the matter with you? Are you stupid or something? (Disrespect)

Assistant to manager: Look, I can accept that the report needs revision, but I feel disrespected when you insult me. (Step 1)

The manager could make one of two responses. First, the rational response.

Manager: I'm sorry. I shouldn't do that, but I'm feeling overwhelmed.

Assistant: Okay, let's get back to the report and solve the problem.

Now, the irrational response.

Manager: You are too sensitive. (Disrespect in the form of subtle criticism)

Assistant: I don't think I am, but I still feel disrespected when you yell and call me stupid.

The discussion should end at this point. "We can talk about it later" is a good exit line. Hopefully, the discussion will not occur, but if it does, stay with Option One. Do not be pulled into a negotiation about your self-respect.

Wife to husband (complaining tone): Can't you see that this house is a mess? Why are you just sitting there while I'm cleaning up? I go to work, too, you know. (Disrespect)

Husband to wife: Please, do not accuse me of not cooperating. Just ask me to help. It is disrespectful to label me as lazy and unhelpful. (Step 1)

Wife to husband: Look, I have too much to do. That's all.

Husband: Let's do what is necessary now, so we can relax together as soon as possible.

The wife will have one of two responses.

Rational: Okay.

Irrational: I shouldn't have to ask you. You should see that I need help.

At this point, he must end an escalating fight. Leave the room. Give her a hug—do what it takes, but I do not believe in going on talking about emotionally based fights. If your couples counselor advises a "sit down," leave that to the Mafia. Empathy is more powerful than discourse.

Girlfriend 1 to Girlfriend 2 (whining tone, attempt to guilt-trip): I called you three times last night. I was really upset. That guy I was dating didn't call me, and I am going out of my mind. You just ignore me. What kind of friend are you? I am always there for you. (Disrespect)

Girlfriend 2: I know how upset you get, but it is disrespectful to call me a bad friend. I do the best I can, but I need some time to myself. (Step 1)

Girlfriend 1: I can't rely on you or anyone. (Cries and feels sorry for herself.)

Girlfriend 2: I know how upset you get, but it is just disrespectful to call me a bad friend. I really do the best I can, but I do need some time to myself. (Repeats statement and does not sympathize. Eventually, she will be heard. If friend 1 hangs up in anger, call her back within forty-eight hours. If she continues to be irrational, simply repeat your statement.)

Mother to seventeen-year-old: You must complete that project tonight. I will not allow you to watch TV if you don't. And I'll ground you this weekend. You are so irresponsible. I mean it! (Disrespect)

Teenager: Mom, I am responsible for my work and when I complete it. I feel disrespected when you try to micromanage my life. Give me a chance to prove to you that I can be responsible. (Step 1)

Mother: Look, I got a call from your teacher two weeks ago about unfinished work. I don't trust your empty promise. (Disrespect)

Teenager: I know, and I was wrong. But I am still responsible for my work and when I complete it. I feel disrespected when you try to micromanage my life. Give me a chance to prove to you that I can be responsible. (Repeats statement. He will get through to her if he is both responsible and insists on respect. Remember, as we train our brains with the Winning Hand of Comfort we train others to respect us.)

The mother can respond in two ways, rational or irrational.

Rational: I want you to be responsible, and I believe you will.

Irrational: No way! There is no way I can trust you.

Teenager: Well, I know you will need some reassurance. What would you suggest?

If the other (in this case, the teenager's mother) is still irrational, offer reassurance anyway: proof of work completed; a call from a teacher, something to buy you credibility, but do not allow overintrusiveness.

Pushy guy to young woman on second date: Mmm, let's make love. I am very attracted to you. You are so sexy. I'll use protection. It's safe. What's the harm? Are you frigid or are you just stringing me along? (Disrespect)

Young Woman: I have told you, I like you but I do not have sex with guys I have just met. I feel disrespected when you call me frigid and manipulative. Just accept my position. (Step 1)

Guy: Sorry, but you look so sexy. You can appreciate that I feel frustrated.

Woman: Yes, but I do not have sex with guys I have just met. I feel disrespected when you call me frigid and manipulative. Just accept my position. (Repeats statement)

The guy can respond in two ways.

Rational (which I think is more likely): Okay. I understand. Let's get together soon.

Irrational: I don't think you mean it. I think you are a teaser.

Young Woman: If you don't trust what I say at this stage, I doubt that we will have a third date.

That's enough. After exercising Option One once and repeating yourself once or, if necessary, twice, *stop*. Your mission was to ask for respect, that's all. Do not expect an apology. Do not expect agreement with your position. Do not necessarily expect respect. *You are making a request, not issuing a command*, and it will be heard even if it is not acknowledged.

Say no more. Confident adults can make a point diplomatically without firing up a conflict. Kids, whose absolute thinking results in concrete, direct, and exaggerated statements ("You are mean! I hate you!"), are not taken seriously. Imply that you want respect.

If you feel insulted or criticized, a simple question can often clarify the situation and invite respect. Say, "I feel insulted by what you said. Did you intend to insult me?" Remember to question the other's intentions unless the insult is clear and obvious.

Maintain a calm tone, a clear statement, and *say no more*. Do not discuss your request. Let it hang in the air. The notion that it is good to talk about why respect is a sound idea is an unsound idea. It makes no sense and a "how could you do this to me—you don't get it" argument is likely to ensue.

Anger propels us to overcome a threat and gain submission—just as war does, by definition. But war is inevitable only when negotiation fails. On the other hand, conflict resolution involves a two-stage agenda: (1) request respect, and (2) resolve the conflict by not taking part in it. Strangers, who don't know you and feel less secure (as they cannot figure out your next move), are more likely to back off and cooperate. Friends, family, and people you work with know you better. They will be slower to change their old ways of responding to you. But don't give up. Never say that you or others cannot change.

EMPATHY: WHAT IS IT?

Empathy is a word that came into common parlance in my flower-child, miniskirted phase in the seventies. When used as psychobabble spin, the word is often misinterpreted and given an unfortunate wimpy, warm-and-fuzzy feel, as if understanding someone would force us to accept and embrace everything a person says or does. Actually, empathy is a solid idea. A confident person needs to be skilled in conveying empathy to others. Some confusion exists as to the meaning of the term, so here is what empathy really means.

I will begin with an empathy quiz. I will describe a conflict my husband and I regularly had in the first years of our marriage. It always occurred at bill-paying time.

RICHARD: We have to cut back on spending. You spend too much. I don't know where we are going to get the money to pay all these bills.

SHEENAH: It's not true! You have no idea what some women spend. I am not the problem. I work hard and I make money. I don't want to hear you complaining all the time.

He blamed me for spending too much money and for not taking our financial problems seriously. I blamed him for complaining and for his ongoing worry about not having enough money, which I knew couldn't be true. In time, we stopped the blaming that had escalated our angry fights by empathically trying to understand what the other was thinking and feeling.

What do you think was behind our anger? Let's start with Richard.

Obviously, he felt angry. What was beneath his anger? It was a shame-based fear of not being able to pay the bills (although I knew this wasn't the reality). Was he feeling sorry for himself and blaming his "spendthrift" wife? Yes, but his wife was not a spendthrift and earned money. So it makes no sense; it is a psychological, not a logical, explanation. Let's continue to look beneath his anger and self-pity. Do you recognize his shame, his embarrassment—a loser feeling? A hint: His late father valued self-sufficiency, but truly struggled to earn a living.

Now let's look at what was beneath my anger. What was I feeling that made me so angry with him? I felt sorry for myself, to be falsely accused and unappreciated by a whiny spouse. And I also value self-sufficiency. I was proud that I could make a significant contribution to the family finances after not working for so long while the children were young. Richard was not acknowledging any of this. Further, despite the financial downturns I experienced with my first husband, I was much less fearful. But in a self-centered way, I disliked Richard's concerns, which didn't always make sense to me. I felt sorry for myself and angrily resented his complaining and what I thought was a lack of consideration. I had had these same feelings before: My first husband's disregard for economy and Richard's promotion of frugality had the same effect on me.

As we came to understand each other better—his fear that he would feel shame if he were a not "good enough provider," and my self-pity for being criticized and misunderstood—we ceased blaming, and our anger and our fights stopped. We calmed ourselves down and comforted each other. We followed what have become golden rules in our own lives and in our practices. When others are upset or angry, do not offer advice or criticism. Unasked-for advice is criticism in disguise, and can ignite anger.

Empathy works better. But to have empathy does not mean you act as a shrink to others. (As you now know, shrinks have irrational fights, too.) Empathy is only an attempt to make sense of others' anger and other feelings, so that you can respond calmly to them. By taking the position of the other person in your mind, you'll be able to explain to yourself why people might act in ways that do not make sense at the time. Explanations are not excuses for bad behavior, but they help us to avoid blaming while conveying our concerns.

Empathy is definitely not sympathy. Do not offer sympathy to people who feel sorry for themselves, unless they are dealing with real threats or losses. Even then, sympathy should be offered only for a short while. Why? Because sympathy weakens the resolve of victims—they will be influenced by you to believe that they are truly helpless—and most people are not truly helpless. Who benefits from hearing, "You poor thing. It's all too much for you"? How demeaning! Some years ago, Richard lost his job as vice president of a small college in Iowa that went bankrupt. He knew the end was coming and had accepted it stoically until people began to offer sympathy. "This is terrible. I wouldn't want to be in your shoes. What are you going to do? These are hard times." In the face of these comments, his realistic acceptance of this interruption to his career disappeared. He began to feel sorry for himself, and hopeless about the future, and slipped into depression. Fortunately, unemployment also gave him time to think through his situation. He realized that well-wishers were killing his spirit with kindness, and that he had an opportunity to make his mark in the field of psychotherapy, which he did.

Let's be frank: Blame is blind.

Let's be clear: Empathy encourages understanding.

THE VICTIM'S REVOLT

Managing anger means taking the high road alone. We alone are responsible for managing our feelings and the manner in which we express them. Everyone else has the same responsibility. Confident people do not feel sorry for themselves, and they do not claim that others are responsible for their plight.

When life seems to turn against us, one of two things has occurred. One, it is a *normal reversal*—an upsetting but common event that most people have experienced or will experience: the loss of opportunity, a deep disappointment or worse, the death of a loved one.

Two, it is a *self-defeating act*. When trouble erupts, we mostly have a hand in it. There are few 100 percent accidents. When we can look at ourselves honestly and without blame, and accept that we alone created our shame and self-pitying reaction, we can then understand and rectify our errors and habits, and grow in confidence and competence. Let me repeat this important message: *Every act of self-control is an act of self-respect.*

"But Sheenah," you might ask, "I don't get angry—well, hardly ever. I am not a bully or a troublemaker. I prefer to make peace and avoid trouble. My problem is anxiety. I fear anger and avoid upsetting people. I hate to offend. I try to be a nice person." Well, I will tell you, everyone gets angry, but some of us were raised to feel guilty and ashamed of being angry. Upsetting others was a serious offense in some families. Remember, my own mother told me that if I couldn't say anything nice I should not say anything at all. Being passive puts us at the mercy of others' wishes or our view of them. We will not easily say no, and sometimes we even hide our opinions for fear of causing disagreement.

This loser policy definitely causes resentment (anger) and self-pity, but if your anger is hidden even from you, you will feel anxiety—a sense of pressure in your chest area. Some passive people have panic attacks, which I believe are covert temper tantrums.

Search your brain for what you are angry about. Rifle through the random items you are worrying about. Our brains are like a dresser drawer, full of a variety of items. Look for those that displease you, upset you, or are just not the way they should be. They are the key to your anger.

You now know that people who feel sorry for themselves tend to feel helpless and those who feel shame tend to feel hopeless. These feelings lead to resentment and anger. Your anxiety and stress-related physical symptoms are direct responses to your inability to manage feelings. It is time to shake up the old way and rebel against your old passive, avoiding habit. Remember, confidence is your mission statement—this is what you signed up for. So, work through the Winning Hand of Comfort after you recognize your anger.

DEALING WITH COMPLAINERS, BLAMERS, AND THOSE WITH RIPPED-OFF DISORDER

"But Sheenah, don't you agree that I need to be assertive, outspoken, and say what's on my mind?" No, that's not a good idea. I had assertiveness training years ago, and I discovered that it turned me into a bully. Bullies are never confident, and they offend others. I consider assertiveness to be immature and self-centered. "You have rights," I was told. It was never clear to me just exactly what these rights were. These workshops I attended were taught by counselors and feminists who cited neither legal nor philosophical bases for the rights they insisted I had. It seemed to me that I could, in my self-centered way, invent rights for myself at will and demand that others comply with them.

How should you respond when you become the target of punitive, sulky, self-pitying indirect anger? Well, Option Three, the most confident move of all, is a good beginning (see page 201). Remember that sulking self-pitiers much prefer to blame others than to shame (criticize) themselves. A person who easily feels victimized by others has a passive-aggressive anger habit. They suffer from what I call "Ripped-off Disorder." It takes very little to set them off. "I can't find my keys. Someone has taken them!" "Don't be too friendly, others will take advantage of you." "I've lost my _____, who moved it?"

So what should you say when passively bullied? Never confront passive-aggressives directly. If you comment on their dark mood you will meet a wall of denial: "I'm fine" or a snappy "Just leave me alone." Live through the discomfort of the silent treatment by comforting yourself for a while. Anger diffuses, and sulkers know they are not behaving kindly, but pride prevents them from cracking the deep freeze they created.

Sometime later—you decide when—just try changing the subject in a cheerful way. This provides a way out from the anger, guilt, and pride cycle the withdrawn person is in. If you feel mad at me now because I advise against punishing the punisher, just think what happens when you do—more anger, more time wasted sulking, and a real possibility that you will go through a hostile standoff time and time again.

A footnote here: If a partner, lover, or spouse is a sulker and acts very independently during their dark periods, don't beg or cry, plead or cajole. If there is something your partner usually does for you, do it yourself. Cook a meal, collect the cleaning. If purposeful lateness is their punishment of choice, leave for an appointment without him or her, after giving a kind reminder. Never indulge a passive-aggressive. Without punitive impact there is no point in their continuing to punish you.

After the storm has passed and the anger defused, refuse to discuss the event or any of the long litany of past wrongs passive-aggressives love to store as evidence of how you victimized them. It will be tempting, but deny yourself the chance to set them straight. How *you* act, behave, and respond in an angry situation bears *no* discussion. I do not believe that others reform because we talk about them. An invitation, such as "let's talk about it," often sets off another round of the same fight. In the fast-moving world of anger, words speak louder than actions, but a comforting, calming presence needs no language, no retribution, or empty apology. Calm, comforting confidence is very catching. So distribute it widely the next time anger comes your way.

Do not blame a blamer. Counter their irritating accusations with those delicious miniescape words and phrases that sound as if they have meaning but don't. Here are some examples:

- "Oh, really?"
- "Is that the case?"
- "I really don't know."
- "I'll give some thought to what you said."
- "I have no idea."
- "What an interesting perspective."

These are all acid reducers that will cut down on bile and end an angry eruption of hot air. Let's put this into practice.

"I cannot find my handbag. Did you take it?"

"No."

"Well, someone did."

"Oh, really?"

Say no more.

"I don't think you should trust those people (professionals from

THE PROBLEM WITH ANGER   213

the dry cleaner to the investment company, your boss, your neighbor, etc.); they are ripping you off."

"*What an interesting perspective.*"

Say no more.

Changes like these build confidence, for now you can manage anger in these tough situations. But be warned: This new way will meet with resistance because of the powerful pull of habit. We are familiar with our relationships to each other. However upsetting at times, we are unlikely to change them easily. This is why people have the same fight over and over again. The content hardly matters, and often the parties cannot even recollect it. They are merely attached to the struggle.

Expect the people you know to try to push you back into being the old you they know so well. Here's what might happen—be prepared:

- More insults and disrespectful criticisms, including, "You're crazy"—a popular and inaccurate way to explain away our stepping out of character
- More arguments about your being wrong and the other person being right. (Remember that it takes two to argue and *you* don't have to.)
- More bullying or whining
- More temper tantrums and tears, aimed at restoring the old unconfident you through either intimidation or guilt

My clients tell me that spouses who express anger immaturely will often say similar things when they come up against their partners' new request for respect: "Is that your shrink talking?" or "If that Sheenah person could see how you treat me she would give you better advice." They have difficulty attributing a respect-seeking action to the person they know. Because it is inconsistent with past behavior, they claim that rather than a new voice of your own, you must be merely parroting me. Refuse to feel annoyed with the accusation that you are merely my passive disciple. Instead, say, "I wanted to speak up long ago, and I have finally made a decision to do so."

You'll build confidence by managing your anger when confronted with a sulky, passive-aggressive style. Remember, sulkers blame others for their problem. They feel sorry for themselves. Say nothing to them, and calm and comfort yourself. Anger dissipates and diffuses with time. Sulkers long to get out of their funk, so sometime later, reach out and act as if nothing had happened. "Would you like a cup of tea?" or some other kind suggestion may do the trick.

"But Sheenah, this is giving in," you may tell me. No, it is resolving conflict. Do not punish the punisher. In time, after many rounds of Option Three, showing empathy, they'll shorten their sulking and replace it with more mature exchanges. Give it time. Always be empathic to others' angry, self-defeating traps. Feeling guilty and ashamed of their own angry, immature behavior, many people try to find a way out of the conflict that is not necessarily honest and straightforward. Do not attempt to correct them, for confident people follow a *no-advice, no-criticism* policy whenever possible. Just listen to their face-saving excuses and declarations:

- "Come on, get off my back. I've had a tough day."
- "Look, you know I love you. So I get upset. So what? I get over it fast."
- "I believe in holding my assistants' feet to the fire. They perform for me."
- "I am not a morning person."
- "You've got to understand, I'm not an uptight person. I show my feelings."
- "I'm tired. Leave me alone."

I encourage you not to sympathize with any of these excuses—just let it go. No arguing. Simply allow the face-saving statement and assume that feelings of guilt and shame are there even if they are not spoken out loud. Keep up a new calm and confident approach to resolving your disrespect problem and you will win. As I said, be patient. The effort will improve your confidence and build more trusting, resilient, confidence-inspiring relationships in the long run.

You can succeed at revolutionizing your anger style through persistent rehearsal, and there is an extra incentive. As you change yourself through persistent practice, others will change, too. If anyone—friend, partner, or (worse), counselor or psychotherapist—trots out that old, ill-thought-out cliché "You can't change other people," disagree! We are continually influencing others and getting influenced by them. If you change, so will others around you, or else they will drop out of your life. As you grow in confidence, others will catch the good bug, too.

I cannot change my curly hair inherited from my Danish Viking ancestors, but I have changed my level of confidence, and this changed everything. It heightened my ambition, encouraged me in my efforts, and made me a more empathic, loving, and accepting wife and mother (and a more powerful therapist). I wish I could have achieved this earlier in my life, but I struggled to get there and I want you to do the same thing, as many of my clients have.

A young man felt like giving up on life. It's all torment, he believed. He described himself as incompetent, indecisive, and ashamed. His well-intentioned mother had an extreme yet unconscious habit of inviting her son to be mad at her by calling him up every day and giving advice and criticism as if he were still a little boy. Although he was twenty-something and smart, he was confused and did not listen to or trust his own judgment. Despite his dependence on her views, he resented her calls.

Here is how he described his mother: "She treats me as someone who needs to be directed, worried over, tutored, doctored, helped, shamed, pressured, corrected, protected, and mentored. She has no regard for my experience or my desire to shape my own self-worth. She wants to fix me from the outside."

I suggested that his mother might be persuaded to desist from this bullying, managerial way of treating him. His reply: sighs of hopelessness. "It's useless. She won't listen. She is so kind to me in every way, I would just feel too guilty and ashamed of myself if I hurt her."

Mother and son had an immature attachment. She treated him as if he were six, and emotionally he felt like a six-year-old. He felt too dependent on his mom to insist on respect and to risk trusting himself. He felt that his confidence was at an all-time low. Both were enraged; she openly, if he dared to disagree with her; he silently, trying when he could to avoid her dreaded telephone calls, e-mail messages, and useless articles about how he should live his life.

After a time, he learned to play with a Winning Hand. He stopped trusting his guilty, self-pitying feelings and actively tried to change himself *and her*. Without discussion of any kind, he calmly insisted that she give him no advice or criticism. Once a week, they could exchange family news and chat. At first she argued, accused, and complained, trying to guilt-trip him into changing his mind and complying with her wishes. "What is a mother for, if not to help?" she wept. He especially needed to use the Winning Hand of Comfort to get through this tough time.

He was never sure what happened or if she really understood, but after repeating the message over many weeks, one evening he walked into my office with a broad grin on his face. "I feel like Henry Higgins," he said, referring to the musical *My Fair Lady*. "I think she's got it."

Managing your own anger and knowing how to respond to anger from others is an essential task, for anger is everywhere, and defending one's self-respect against insult is a key to confidence.

A confident person values close relationships and builds strong connections with others. Rugged individualism has been overvalued in Western culture. A do-your-own-thing, march-to-your-own-drummer theme has been promoted at the expense of a focus on respectful, supportive social relationships.

Self-centered expressions of anger will drive us apart. By confidently managing anger, we inspire self-respect and promote self-confidence and confidence in others. In this way, anger can be a constructive agent for change.

Let's be frank: You can change others if you change yourself.

Let's be clear: Anger is a great gift. It protects you. Use it sparingly, and with confidence.

NINE

ANXIETY: THE CONFIDENCE KILLER

We all hear voices, but that does not mean we are crazy. The Irish writer Nuala O'Faolain was filled with anxiety rather than delight when her publisher invited her to write about herself as an introduction to a collection of her essays. She describes her experience in her memoir *Almost There*:

"From the instant, I had to fight with inner voices that mocked my self-importance. 'You aren't helping me get through life!' I shouted back at them."

Anxiety gives constant voice to the fearful. Inside the mind, an ongoing rattle of warning and command clamors: Don't take chances, avoid people—they may dislike you. Danger stalks, like a lurking serial killer, on the lookout for its next victim. It will crash an airplane, suck the air out of any small space, burn down your house, and bring sickness and even death to your children. Its message pours acid on your confidence, and it awaits your next idea, hope, and enterprise, so that it may finish it off before you triumph. I have a way to kill it, and we must start now, for your confidence is under siege.

The spectrum called fear splits into many anxious colors: the vivid green of envy, the pale yellow of cowering cowardice, the inflaming red of jealousy, and the frozen whiteness of fear. Transparent ectoplasm of nervousness ebbs and flows, breaking up and taking form, like tiny amoebas of worry that engulf an image of a person, a dark prediction or a disastrous fantasy, and give them life. These freefloating pinpoints of fear eventually dissipate and dissolve back into the ever-present jellylike mass of quivering anxiety.

Perhaps you remember, as I do, your first full-blown anxiety experience. My chest remembers, too: Even now it is tightening and my lungs, reluctant to go along with my memory, are making it slightly more difficult for me to breathe. My heart seems madly out of control. It beats against my chest, a protester loudly making its views known. Look here, they say, we struggle night and day to keep you going. Why put us under this pressure? It's not fair.

The excitement of anxiety drives roller-coaster riders, Nascar drivers, extreme-sports enthusiasts, and everyday sports fans who shout at TVs at home and in bars when their guys win or lose. We love the feeling of this form of anxiety we call excitement. But no one loves panicky anxiety, the intense excitation that seems to come out of the blue, scaring us into temporary disability. Trembling, unable to think clearly, it's as if we watch our scared bodies overreact. Too much emotion jumbles our brains. Why? Is this a heart attack? What is happening to me?

The function of anxiety is protection. We experience anxiety as a physical sensation that drives body muscles to tense and brain "muscles" to focus with vigilant concern. All living things respond this way when faced with a threat. The sensation of fear is instantaneous and without pause, for the brain reacts in a protective fashion, so we rush to safety when faced with a threat, or freeze and hope to go unnoticed.

Let's be frank: Anxiety is fear.

Let's be clear: Fear is anxiety.

There are three basic types of anxiety, which I'll briefly describe.

While everyone may experience them from time to time, they are not problems for confident people, who know how to manage their feelings.

1. Social anxiety
2. Paranoid anxiety
3. Anxiety about anxiety

Social Anxiety

Philip Zimbardo, a prominent psychologist, has studied shyness for over twenty-five years. He reported in 1975 that 40 percent of American college students considered themselves to be shy. They suffered from social anxiety—fears of embarrassment and anxiety about potential criticism and conflict. If you were to study children between the ages of about eighteen months and sixteen years of age, you would find that nearly 100 percent of them would have some degree of social anxiety, for this is a natural, immature response in the vulnerable young. Even the boldest child and the most rebellious teenager take criticism, censure, and penalty very seriously when it is delivered by a respected and therefore feared source. They seek approval from a respected authority figure, for the young are essentially powerless and rely on mature, powerful adults for protection, rational guidance, and psychological comfort.

The mixed feelings of anxious neediness and resentment are the main reasons that adolescence is difficult. Adults who have not taken the step to mature independence rely on others for approval, affirmation, reassurance, and comfort.

Social anxiety is fear of other people's scrutiny, and of their judgments. It is the fear that somehow we won't measure up to their expectations and will be criticized. Of course, if we didn't take people's judgments so seriously, we wouldn't fear them. When we do take them seriously, we silently nod in agreement with those judgments—judgments we mostly imagine. We become anxious in anticipation of being judged for appearing inadequate or foolish, and this anxiety prompts us to avoid, whenever we can, social situations in which we might be unfavorably scrutinized.

"I blush like a beet. I get tongue-tied, and then I am so embarrassed by the silent pauses that I babble on about nothing. I go home and beat myself up for the dumb things I said." Leah was describing how she typically reacted to a situation she found so threatening that she had avoided it for over a year: dating. "What am I going to do? I'm thirty-six, and I want to get married and have kids, but I hate the way dating makes me feel."

At that moment, Leah did not know what you know—that she was so self-critical that she falsely believed that any man, even a stranger she hardly knew, would be critical of her also. She felt anxious about feeling embarrassed, and avoided both feelings by not dating. "I certainly would prefer my perfect guy just to show up and marry me," she confided. Together, we established four goals for her:

- To stop criticizing herself
- To stop believing that everyone was a critic as she was
- To apply the Winning Hand of Comfort to manage her anxiety
- To accept that she must increase her confidence by facing what she feared

Dates became target practice—just a simple, straightforward opportunity to take aim at anxiety. To help divert her attention from her own feelings, I asked her to focus on the guy and on whether he seemed suitable for *her*. "You mean I should think about whether he's good enough for me, instead of how I'll blow it by saying something stupid?" she asked. "Yes," I said, "you don't know what he thinks of you, so concentrate on what you think of him, and don't assume that he's the last available decent man in the world." (The "last good man on earth" theory is one I often hear but never agree with.)

Still blushing and stumbling over her words, Leah stopped avoiding and began to date. She was surprised to discover that her nervousness did not lead to automatic rejection. In fact, anxiety is a feeling others can empathize with, and empathy can make us feel closer to each other.

A year or so, and many dates, later, she came to see me. She carried a bridal magazine with several pages marked up. "Look, I know I am a lot more confident in most areas of my life—I wouldn't be getting married if I weren't—but I feel indecisive about choosing my wedding dress. Which do you like?" I offered an opinion, but I knew she would make a fine choice without my help. Leah's anxiety was in check, and planning her wedding was a dream she had made a reality, but her anxiety habit lingered a little; it was too familiar to her to simply vanish. When there was nothing to worry about, she found something to stress over, such as her dress decision. "Comfort yourself," I reminded her. "You can make the right decision." She did, and her wedding pictures proved it.

Of the 50 percent of Americans who deem themselves shy, only 15 to 20 percent fit our concept of a shy person—nervous, withdrawn, head hung down, and ill at ease in company—according to a study by psychologist Paul Pilkonis. The great majority is internally shy. Many are openly entertaining and seem socially comfortable, but like comedians and clowns through the ages, an internal drama of self-doubt is occurring. (Do I sound smart? Am I entertaining? Do they like me? Will they laugh at my jokes?) They rely on pleasing or entertaining others to alleviate anxiety.

Finally, do not overlook the likelihood that self-pity accompanies and strengthens social anxiety. You may feel sorry for yourself for avoiding social situations that might be enjoyable ("It's not fair. I'm shy. Why do I have to go?"). You may feel victimized by needy people who want your attention and by demanding people who want your time ("Why can't they leave me alone?").

Paranoid Anxiety

This sounds like a clinical term, but it isn't. I created the label to separate social anxiety, which leads to avoidance, from fear of bad things happening, which leads to excess caution and wariness. In social anxiety, other people are the victimizers; in paranoid anxiety, things or events are the victimizers.

Anxiety based on a prediction of potential victimization is a powerful emotional magnet. Given a choice between all potential outcomes, an anxious mind focuses only on threatening thoughts, mostly imaginary ones. These are the straight steel pins that will prick you if you are not careful. Watch out! Beware! What if disaster lurks around the corner? These pins are drawn and polarized by an anxiety magnet that feels as if it were implanted in the thymus (upper midchest). They pin you down and prevent you from making confident moves and warn you that you must not rely on others to do their part. They prick your memory, dredging up negative past experiences.

Fear of being victimized reaches its zenith in paranoid people, who imagine that there are enemies out there, waiting to hurt them. In extreme cases, groups of conspiracy theorists surround every tragedy with a cloak of plot and suspicion. They promote mistrust of the government, banks, the world, the rich, and the poor. This endless list of potential enemies is described in ways that contain a germ of truth, just enough to make it sound as if the paranoia might be based on fact alone. In reality, these paranoid anxious beliefs are damned with faint logic.

However, this extreme anxiety habit is rare. Minor paranoia is much more prevalent, even more pervasive. Many untrusting people believe that the world is a threatening, dangerous place, and that most people are likely to disadvantage or rip them off in some fashion, if they get the chance. In a single week, I see many people with Ripped-off Disorder; their self-pity addiction is supported by a habit of mistrust and negative prediction. ("I must be vigilant, compulsive, and must worry, or I will be ripped off.") At first they are stubborn when I point out that their feelings, not people and the world, are the problem. They refuse to recognize their self-pity for fear of seeming weak, whiny, and complaining. I point out that in life, nothing much happens most of the time. "What did you do a week ago last Tuesday?" I ask. "I don't know—just a regular day," is the typical reply. So their fear is inside, not outside, and they begin to understand my point.

I confess to exaggerating the word "paranoid" on purpose. My hyperbole is a stop sign to the mistrustful, who self-centeredly believe the world is a critical, condemning place where censure is the rule. This belief is not true. Shame at making "wrong decisions" creates the potential for self-pity and the anxiety of needing to be right. Those with this form of paranoid anxiety immaturely seek a lot of advice, in their quest for the perfect right answer. They seek it as though it were the Scarlet Pimpernel—they seek it here, they seek it there, they hunt for an answer everywhere, but it remains elusive.

People with paranoid anxiety often resort to being overly careful, and they may indulge in compulsive behaviors as a source of comfort. Every such person I worked with had chronic anxiety based on an ongoing fear—of being criticized and victimized by life. A "germ phobic" sees dirt as proof that microscopic enemies lie in wait, ready to deliver poisons and infections. Frequent hand washing and disinfecting ward off these terrorists; of course, the threat does not really exist, so cleansing rituals are simply ways to reduce anxiety—temporarily. "Did I turn off the gas? Did I lock the door?" Repetitive checking wards off disastrous anxiety, but only for the moment. The feeling quickly returns.

We have all met the supertidy folk who live in pristine homes. They always appear to be dry-cleaned, blow-dried, and manicured. They can always find everything in their pocketbooks, and never lose their glasses or car keys. They can be relied upon never to forget your birthday (even when you want to) or anything else. They may command our admiration and perhaps envy, yet many of these folks are highly anxious and fear shameful censure. They will go to great lengths to seek some kind of perfection, so that you and everyone else will be approving (or at least not disapproving).

But let's be frank: There is no comfort in completion. Why? Because the hours it takes to create a polished, perfect environment are a prison sentence of time wasted on minutiae and worry about maintenance. Tiredness is a real problem for compulsive cleaners and fixers.

So of course they fail in these fatiguing, overly time-consuming pursuits. The world is an untidy place—leaves fall, bugs eat patches of grass, and moles dig up the lawn. To a degree, clean enough but untidy is normal and does not disturb the confident person. However, on the other side of the spectrum are those who procrastinate instead of completing the incredibly tedious tasks of self-care and housekeeping. If your life is so messy that your desk is piled high, you can't get into bed because of all the stuff on top, and there is a lot of unwashed underwear strewn around, then you create shame and anxiety by procrastinating about necessary and essential tasks of self-care and housekeeping. Brilliantly, you generate much shame and self-pity by being the victim of messy stuff. Should someone come to call, (social) anxiety barrels in, and you apologize in advance for the mess or do not let them in.

Let's be frank: People pursue security, not happiness.

Let's be clear: Anxiety and vigilance do not promote security. Anxiety begets anxiety.

Anxiety About Anxiety

This term refers to the fearful anticipation of experiencing anxiety—to having those tense and panicky feelings we know as "anxiety." It is the number one reason people who want to make changes in their lives fail to do so. We can conquer almost every fear by doing what we fear. But the discomfort we must go through in order to do so stops us all too often. No wonder people seek counseling and psychotherapy—

and take tranquilizing medications—in the hope that they can feel less afraid and *then* do what they fear. None of us, including myself, likes to feel uncomfortable, but there are times when we should put up with it, in order to get where we want to go.

Anxiety is the opposite feeling from confidence. While a person who is truly confident may feel some apprehension or uneasiness from time to time, it is unthinkable that anxiety and confidence can coexist within the same person. Lack of confidence and the feeling of anxiety are for all practical purposes the same.

If you avoid taking action because you fear feeling anxious, you are hamstringing your confidence. I have met people who will not fly in a plane, swim in the sea, entertain at home, flirt with a person they are attracted to, or have easygoing, comfortable afternoon sex. What scares them? Crashes, sharks, drowning, being criticized as a lousy hostess, or being deemed as less than a good lover? No, not really. It is their *predictions* of how scared and embarrassed they will feel that fill them with anxiety. I met a young woman who was about to be married. She was really scared of having children. Why? She lived in dread of throwing up. I helped her to comfort her anxiety, for our bodies deliver a baby without much intervention from us. Our bodies will quickly empty our stomachs of noxious substances, without intervention from us. Anxiety is different; it is a habit and it requires a strong, determined, persistent intervention—the Winning Hand of Comfort. Over time and with practice, I promise you that your body and your brain will learn, and your anxiety will be taken care of without intervention from you.

ANXIETY AS A HABIT

If anxiety (fear) were only a real or imagined danger, it would be quite easy to understand and remedy. But there is more to it than that. Throughout *Complete Confidence* I have discussed feelings as *habits*, not just reactions.

People who come from families in which anxiety was frequently felt experience habitual anxiety. It is a familiar feeling for them, and therefore one that will be sought out from time to time. And at such times, their confidence will be shaken. This is most likely to occur when things have been going well and confidence couldn't be higher. Deprived of the familiar feeling of anxiety, such a person will create situations in which to feel anxious and/or imagine (real or social) dangers to fear. I call the people I have just described "anxiety seekers."

Don't equate them with "thrill seekers"—folks who seek out challenges, usually physically dangerous ones, for the rush or thrill they provide. Thrill seekers take risks most of us avoid. They jump from airplanes, climb mountains, and try new experiences just for the hell of it. Far from lacking confidence, they are usually very confident people, and know how to handle the anxiety we all feel at times.

A CASE OF MISTAKEN IDENTITY

The sensations of tension that we usually label "anxiety" may instead be due to another emotion: anger. Our bodies experience these sensations in very similar ways—a physical tension often to the point of trembling, feeling flushed, and breathing irregularly. A minor celebrity I know recalled a moment of intense "anxiety," which he called a "panic attack," when he was recognized in a store by another customer. Upon further discussion, I discovered that he was not afraid, and therefore wasn't anxious; rather, he was angry that the customer intruded on his privacy, and he was angry with himself that he was only a minor celebrity—in his mind, he thought he should have achieved much more.

These so-called panic attacks often involve anger. Many counselors and psychologists and journalists who write in magazine articles about panic and anxiety disorders overlook the element of blame, the driving force of anger. Through useless, unproductive blame, we attempt to point the shame finger away from ourselves in order to gain relief for a while. Our emotionally overloaded brain—unable to calm itself—panics.

A TURNING POINT

For two years or so, ending in late summer 2000, I became a regular trans-Atlantic traveler. About every eight weeks, in the late evening, I would leave my office for New York's JKF Airport and catch a British Airways flight to London's Gatwick Airport. I wheeled my small weekend bag and lugged a heavy case of anxiety. In my head, I just wanted to go home as usual. A preoccupying worry filled my mind and made me forgetful. It took away my normal concentration. I knew I must double-check my passport, tickets, and reading glasses, too. I knew where the familiar departure gates were, but somehow could not fully remember. I would wander through the overlit, lonely jail of the departure lounge and ask the benevolent jailers in uniform where I must go and what I must do. Sometimes I asked more than once, for anxiety purposefully short-circuits our thinking so we can make fast escapes.

Sleep was usually impossible despite my fatigue. Anxiety is an emotion that urges us not to relax, but to take action, to effect an escape plan. Trapped in my narrow coach seat, all I could feel were waves of fearful anticipation about what lay ahead upon my arrival, which I faced up to with my usual well-practiced comfort phrase. Then I felt calmer, and was in better shape to deal with what I knew was likely to be a serious threat.

Landing at Gatwick in the very early hours, I noted the familiar half-light of southern England. As usual, a low gray sky and bone-chilling rain welcomed me. Their welcome matched my mood—irritable, resentful, anxious, and a little sorry for myself. I turned my rental car south, sensing an increasing dread building in my chest and throat. I so wanted to go north and race upcountry to my old home in the Midlands, to the comfort and kindness of friends and family who still live there.

In the early dawn, I drove nervously down the M25 into the unfamiliar limestone downs of Kent and Sussex, past exits marked with the names of towns I did not recognize, whose churches, pubs, and grocery stores I had never set foot in. I tried to distract myself by imagining the lives of the other drivers, my companions on this lonely morning drive on an unusually quiet motorway. My destination was a newish brick complex set tidily in a neat parking lot surrounded by standard English flowerbeds. The building was both ominous and anonymous—no one can tell what goes on inside—it could be a corporate office, a small apartment complex, or some obscure government department.

I parked and locked the car, and holding my umbrella walked to the heavy glass entrance doors to the building. I pushed them open, knowing that they would be unlocked despite the early hour. Entrance is possible twenty-four hours a day, if you know the secret code to the computer locks on the second barricaded set of doors inside. My anxiety had begun to rise when an official of this establishment telephoned me in New York. This had never happened before. She instructed me to report to the central office immediately on my arrival. This was unusual, and I found the request scary. My anxiety was now at that weird point when its discomfort outweighed the enormity of the threat, and I wished that the worst would just happen already.

Tense and grave, I sat in the visitor's chair facing a desk in the main office. The woman in charge leaned kindly toward me and made a seemingly simple request that sends a toxic shock through the central nervous system of any British person in a frightening situation. She began by saying, "Would you like a nice cup of tea?" If this is offered prior to impending news, especially if the offer includes the adjective "nice," you just know that what comes next will be nasty. Tea is the herbal Valium, the hot brewed Prozac, the inevitable shot of anesthesia offered when one faces a hopeless situation.

Tense and fearful, I could not form words for several seconds. Then I managed a question, "She's worse, isn't she?" "Much," replied the head nurse of my mother's Alzheimer's unit. "She will not know you anymore. I wanted to warn you before you saw her."

When I did see her some minutes later, she was sitting silently in an armchair next to rows of other female residents, so neat in their cotton dresses, woolly cardigans, and sensible shoes—and so fuzzy and messy in their damaged brains. I did not recognize her at first. Alzheimer's disease is progressive. It cuts everyone down to the same size: thin, small, white-haired, glazed eyes, funny stumbling gait. I wept quietly. Who was this? Was this my mother?

Soon afterward we shared a cup of tea in her room. I held hers for her. Familiar with the unit but not with her daughter, my mother soon got up and without saying a word walked back to her chair in the common room, leaving me alone.

How could this happen so fast? What on earth could I do? Anger and self-pity mixed in with my anxiety and jumbled my thinking. I stared blindly out the window. Suddenly, I spotted something. Under the hedge, a magnificent, wild red fox sat, staring straight at me, unafraid and still. I had noticed him sitting there on my last visit some months before. A suburbanite now, he had not changed: strong, fit, clear-eyed, and magnificent. I felt comforted by my mother's neighbor. Living among the enemy, he sniffed the air unafraid. He knew my mother could not raise an alarm. He could take care of himself. Despite daily threats, he had survived.

And I would survive, too. Anxious feelings had haunted me daily as a young woman. I was too dependent on my mother then for advice and comfort. It had been a long time since I felt that way. The fox was not threatened by her presence; he had no need of her. I recognized in that silent moment that I had finally lost her. The fox and the daughter, both looking at her, were well able to care for themselves. For me, this was a symbolic ending to the relationship between the once immature dependent woman and the mother who raised her.

I am no longer scared, indecisive, and nervous, brilliant at undermining my confidence with shameful, self-pitying predictions about the loss of face, failure, and embarrassment. Not anymore and not to-day. But this loss of my mother was a threat to me and to my children. Our lives had changed. Yet I knew I must handle it confidently with the Winning Hand of Comfort. I went through the steps methodically, grateful that my powerful, single sentence "tranquilizer"—"Sheenah, don't overreact"—was rapidly taken up in my brain's synapses, calming me instantly. This stuff is a lot better than tea, I thought, as I drained my cup and dried my eyes. I had managed infants in the past—four in all—and I would manage my infantilized mother. It was my turn now.

My mother died in the late summer of that year, leaving me the remains of her messy life: a large, crumbling, ill-kept house and a confusing case of "will hell." My anger at her irresponsibility left me wanting to pour money into the hungry mouths of lawyers, like baby formula, just to try to secure some tangible proof of her existence. I often wonder now if the fox is staring with his golden eyes at someone else's mother, whose brain had decided to retire before her body was quite ready to leave. I was glad I had the confidence to manage my feelings.

HOW CONFIDENT PEOPLE MANAGE ANXIETY

After this visit, I decided to do a simple survey. I asked confident people, Do you ever get anxious? What do you worry about? How do you manage your anxiety? There is a clear message that runs through their responses.

- "When I feel anxious I ask myself, 'Does this make sense or not?' If I have a real problem, I decide to stop just brooding about it and do something. Honestly, 95 percent of the time it is solved, and the other 5 percent, so what. I live with it. You can't win them all."
- "You know, I realize that I don't get anxious much, but I say I am anxious when I am angry. For example, I am very punc-

tual. My husband drags his feet and often makes us late. I get tense, but realize I am annoyed with him because I believe it is inconsiderate to others not to be on time. Then I calm down. It's never more than a few minutes. What's the big deal? Why spoil a good time?"

- "Frankly, I like the anxiety. It's always about a business decision. Will I get the deal? Do the numbers work? Will the bank come in with the right support? If it doesn't work, it doesn't work. On to the next. There is always another deal. I suppose I should worry about terrorists or cancer or something, but I take care of myself, so what's the point?"

- "Sure, I get anxious sometimes. About money or some big event. What do I do? I stop and think about what I can do. How can I solve the problem? I feel better when I can think of a solution and put it into action. If I can't solve it, I don't waste my energy worrying."

- "I've trained myself not to worry. I used to worry a lot, especially in the middle of the night. But now, if I begin to feel anxious, worry, I postpone the worry until I can do something. Worry is not the same as problem solving, because there is no solution in worry. So, if I wake up at three a.m., I tell myself to go back to sleep until six or seven, when I can take care of it. Even if I could think of an action at three a.m., whom could I call and what could I do? Everyone else is asleep."

Just in case you missed it, here are the common denominators running through this little survey. Confident people get anxious about *real* problems, not psychological ones. They calm down in order to plan for a solution. They don't get anxious very often. Confident people know when their anxiety is about the breaking of their own personal rules of living, such as lateness, and are not unreasonable when others do not fully share them. (They do not have to be *right* to avoid shame.)

Confident people do not get anxious about anxiety, or invent things to worry about. They actually like the challenges to their competence that a real worry brings to them, as they feel confident in their ability either to solve it or to accept uncritically that they cannot, and move on.

Let's be frank: Confident people don't feel much, most of the time.

Let's be clear: Managing emotions with the Winning Hand of Comfort is the habit of the confident person.

LAYING ON THE WINNING HAND OF COMFORT

If you want to manage your anxiety as confident people do, review the first four steps in the Winning Hand of Comfort: Calm, Clarify, Challenge, Comfort. If your unconscious mind wakes you up in the middle of the night with something you should worry about, don't turn on a TV informercial. Tune your mind to the Winning Hand of Comfort channel. You will see a moving ribbon of information at the bottom of the screen: "Winning Hand of Comfort Step One—calm. Calm the feelings."

Anxious people must slow their breathing. Count the breaths, it always works. This actor's trick instructs the brain to slow down. It will follow your slow breathing lead. Damp down your anxiety so that you can get on to Step Two, the clarification stage.

Clarify: Here is how it works. Ask yourself if you're feeling:

- Anxious (fearful). You may be aware of making future predictions of harmful events or outcomes that will generate familiar feeling habits that undermine confidence.
- Anger at oneself. Blaming thoughts include labeling oneself as Stupid, Fat, Old, Ugly, or a Loser, creating shame, anger at others, at life, at the world.

- Shame. Go deeper and uncover self-criticism and condemnation for feeling Stupid, Fat, Old, Ugly, or a Loser, and behaving in self-defeating ways that are short-term attempts to avoid anxiety, shame, and self-pity.
- Self-pity. Clues to self-pity include bingeing, indulgence as a response to feeling emotionally deprived, whining, and predictions that nothing will get better in the future.

All of the habits on the Second Losing Hand are markers of shame and self-pity that promote anxiety. Look at how others misperceive and label people who Binge, Please, Whine, Procrastinate, and Avoid. Imagine what damage those false assumptions will do to a person's confidence. Remember, people's ideas about each other are simplistic, often judgmental, and blaming.

Challenge. The next step in the Winning Hand of Comfort—Step Three—is very concrete. You must now challenge your thinking. Anxiety and fear are driven by negativity—thoughts that are not about true reality, but verbal coat hangers we can hang our well-worn and familiar feelings upon.

Challenging your thoughts is exactly the right way to argue with yourself. List your thoughts, excuses, justifications, rationalizations, and judgments based, of course, on opinion, not fact. Many of these anxiety-inducing theories are simply inherited, unquestioned propositions that you took on board as you grew up. I will simply take one thought from every finger of both Losing Hands and challenge them, just to show you how.

- Stupid: "I had better not raise my hand and ask a question, I could look stupid." (Losing Hand One, Finger One: Stupid; Losing Hand Two, Finger Five: Avoidance) Challenge: The "stupid" idea is justification for my shame habit. "I didn't do too well in school, but I know now that I was anxious. If I don't ask the question, I will criticize myself (shame). If I don't get heard, my ideas will be ignored (self-pity). With calm and comfort I can and will do it."

- Fat: "I can't control my weight. If I have no food in my fridge I won't overeat." (Losing Hand One, Finger Two: Fat) Challenge: "Food is not my problem, my sense of deprivation is. I am not controlled by food, but by my self-pity habit. Deprive-indulge. I can plan what I will eat and I will eat normally (no diets, unless medically prescribed), but mostly I will calm and comfort my self-pity so I will never need to comfort myself with overeating."

For me, "can't" means "won't." Try making this powerful substitution. In general, confident, mature adults are emotionally self-regulating, which makes life easy much of the time, because they will do what they believe to be right at any given moment, no matter how they feel about this decision.

- Old: "I am too old to look sexy, have sex, etc." (Losing Hand One, Finger Three: Old) Challenge: "Old is a state of mind— a self-pitying feeling, not a fact. I will not give in to this myth. People are never too old."
- Ugly: "I look terrible. Look at this nose, chin, hair." (Losing Hand One, Finger Four: Ugly) Challenge: "I am too critical. Others don't look with my judgmental attitude. I will take care of myself and realize that my negative feelings about myself are catching. If I feel I look good, I'll look out for compliments, for confidence is sexy."
- Loser: "I am just a loser—poor me." (Losing Hand One, Finger Five: Loser) Challenge: *Complete Confidence* taught me that all losers either perceive themselves that way or act irresponsibly and immaturely and make emotional, not rational, decisions. I will strive to do what is right, right now, and not what I feel like doing."

- Bingeing: "I am out of control. I feel compelled to shop (drink, overeat, spend, gamble, etc.)." (Losing Hand Two, Finger One: Bingeing) Challenge: I am not facing the cause of my need to overindulge, my sense of deprivation followed by my powerless complaining—my hopeless self-pity. I will stop believing my complaints and take charge of my feelings by comforting them. I will plan my recovery practically, with help if necessary, starting now.

- Pleasing: "I hate conflict. I like to be liked. I don't know why my efforts to please others cause me to resent them." (Losing Hand Two, Finger Two: Pleasing) Challenge: "I will learn to stand my ground and handle anger. I will read chapter 8 over and over again, so I can rehearse a new response. I will not blame others or myself. I will practice being confident."

- Whining: "Why can't life treat me better? It's not fair! Why don't I get what I want?" (Losing Hand Two, Finger Three: Whining) Challenge: "I do get what I want—a self-pitying, powerless view of myself guilt-trips others into giving me some sympathy, but eventually I get what I don't want—a lot of their anger. I will stop the blame and I will not complain. This will be tough, but every day I will be aware of my whining and stop it."

- Procrastinating: "I will do it tomorrow—mañana—I am unsure about how well I can do it and fear being criticized (shame)." (Losing Hand Two, Finger Four: Procrastinating) Challenge: "I will plan to do it now. I will start within the next few hours. I will ignore everything that is not necessary for me to do. I will carve out a new habit that does not rain shame all over me and invite others' criticism."

- Avoiding: "I don't like parties, I don't like to dance. I look stupid. I don't like to speak in public. I don't like . . ." (Losing Hand Two, Finger Five: Avoidance) Challenge: "I don't have to like being social. These are all emotional decisions. I have to do what I fear in order to be confident, comfortable, and successful. I will start small and comfort my way into all of the nonthreatening situations I have built a wall of fear around."

Comfort. Comfort is the essential adult ingredient that every self-servicing, confident person must acquire. We adults are all highly technical—we program our Palm Pilots, we browse the Internet. We undertake even more complex operations—we drive a car, we paint a room, we bake a casserole, we plan a wedding, we read a book—and it challenges us in some way for the better.

Yet, how many of us know how to comfort our anxiety? Too few, and those who do know how, we admire. They are calm in a storm and confident in their decision making. They see the world as safe and manageable, and they calm their feelings without drugs and addictions. They focus on meeting normal reversals with acceptance and refuse to be held back by them.

Do not be your own terrorizing terrorist. Listen instead to your words of calm and comfort—your chosen phrase that you will imbue with meaning. For the anxious reader, I was once one of your number; my phrase works as well as any: "Sheenah, don't overreact." Please, don't you overreact, either. You can handle it, whatever "it" is.

TEN

A NEW BEGINNING

During the year plus a couple of months that it took me to write this book, I discovered that I had changed. I knew I was a lot of a thinker, but I did not realize that there was a bit of a writer in me. When I reread the first draft of this book, I was surprised to see some glimpses of a writer there.

Writers tell me that they spend a lot of time alone. I did not feel alone, for you, the reader, were here in the room with me all of the time, just like the hundreds of people who have sat on the couch opposite me, in pursuit of confidence. In my practice, I do not have a termination ceremony when clients have achieved what they came for. It is not possible to end an intimate, honest relationship; it is too false and arbitrary. I just leave the door open and I am delighted to hear from former clients. I save pictures of their weddings and new babies, and from afar I relish the confidence they express on notes and holiday cards.

I do believe that I have fulfilled my contract to you and to my publisher, whose confidence in me I appreciate. I have tried to be frank and clear. I hope you understand yourself better now and know what to do with your feelings. You signed on to do your part, and if you are reading this final chapter, this is the last "session" we will spend together. I know you are learning to manage the emotions that blinded you to your potential and have an enduring methodology for comforting any shameful, critical voice and any self-pitying sense of impossibility that will surface. Expect to feel your old feelings from time to time, especially when life is chugging along so well.

When we feel a certain way about ourselves we become very secure with that image in our mind. No matter how fearful and angry we may be; no matter how harshly we lambaste ourselves; and no matter how out of control we feel, we will not recognize how we unknowingly invite the responses from others we are used to getting, even if this causes us ongoing shame and self-pity. We just know ourselves this way. There is security in it. *Complete Confidence* is intended to pry open the lock on that psychological construction of a person and to free the brilliance and the courage that all of us have and were born with.

A young, healthy couple who wants a child has only a 20 percent chance of catching the right moment and then conceiving successfully. This is proof of natural resilience. One vigorous sperm fought its way past millions of almost equally vigorous competitors to father you. An ovum took a long journey and outlasted the onslaughts of negative chemicals to remain fit and fertile, and to be ready to mother you. As a result of the strength shown at the moment of conception, when the odds were stacked against you, you made it and became a cell-dividing organism that grew in nine short months into a feeling, feisty baby who demanded attention immediately, despite an exhausting and bruising trip through a birth canal, which is much too narrow. (For my male readers who may question my criticism of nature's design, check it out with all of the women you know who have succeeded in delivering a baby.)

Not all of us are built to be great risk takers. Our nervous systems may not have the calm resilience present in many airline pilots and astronauts I have read about and listened to. Taciturn, mild-mannered folks, they describe the dramas they face as "just part of the job—all in a day's work." I am often reminded of an old joke about the British habit of emotional understatement: An intrepid explorer, when questioned about his broken arm in a sling, replied, "Just a small fracture. I set it myself."

But many if not most of the clients I know have traumatized nervous systems, brains on high alert for insult and threat, brains that are much better at agitating and alerting them to disrespect, unfairness, embarrassment, and disregard than at comforting anxiety and anger and looking for a management response. Remember, self-critical shame and blaming self-pity are the immature feelings of childhood, a time when others must comfort us or else we do not learn how.

Most of us live in a culture in which raising children is not truly a group activity. Couples and single parents raise children without the daily collective experience of a tight group of grandparents, uncles, aunts, older cousins, and close neighbors. As a result, we are likely either to repeat the limited model of parenting that we grew up with, or if unhappy as a child, do the opposite of what our parent(s) did. So, some children are treated more like pampered pets than people, and grow to be self-indulgent, dependent adults whose natural-born confidence has been usurped by lifelong emotional immaturity. Parents who lack confidence will inevitably pass their emotional habits of fear, shame, and self-pity on, for children pick them up as if by osmosis.

The marvelous advantage of owning a superb human brain is that it is always learning and always making sense of new experiences, changing and adapting in the secret neural pathways we feel but will never see, save in the plastic image of a brain scan.

But be warned: Change is a threat to familiarity and will set off an alarm within. So be careful, for the messages and experiences of childhood are shaped into a model that firms up in adolescence. Stupid is a feeling only. Fat is a feeling only. Old is a feeling. Ugly also. And the term "loser" is the simple, condemning collective noun that sums them all up.

This sense of ourselves orders us into a secure place and instructs us to stay there. Earlier, I called this your emotional set point. Your brain, especially the unconscious part, is a guardian, an adviser, a school monitor with a nagging attitude. This store of emotionally charged memories will be produced if you venture into too confident or too demeaning a place. When you achieve success, just listen for the nagging inner voice: "Who do you think you are? You are reaching beyond your station in life. This can't last—your luck will run out." To prove the point and drive it home, memories flash in: a father who failed, a mother who neglected her children, leaving them afraid of success or unable to expect to shine.

I once worked with a beautiful woman, with long, red hair and bright, unusually green eyes. When she rolled up the sleeve of her fine cashmere sweater, I saw ugly welts on her arm. Later, when she came to trust me, she took off her clothes down to her underwear and revealed a series of bruises and a scar from a cigarette burn. Her husband was a paranoid, jealous man who pathologically believed she was having sex with many men, even with the kindly doormen in her apartment building who were protective toward her. He would punish her, beat her, and later repent, buying her flowers and holding her close as he wept his apologies. He promised never to hurt her again, just as he had for twenty years, but he always broke his promise.

I knew she must leave him, but at first she would only tell me of his good heart, their financial stability, and her fears for her college-age son. She had grown up with two alcoholic parents who would party and fight constantly. As a small girl, she hid under the bed, and she was hiding in a marriage, feeling powerless yet in her own way secure in this familiar arrangement. Filled with silent self-pity and equally silent anger and fear, she could not imagine a better life. She was stuck at her set point, guilty that she could not make her parents happy, or her husband, either.

In time, she learned to comfort her anxiety, guilt, shame, and self-pity. One day in the lobby of her building, after hiring a private security service, she served her husband with divorce papers and an order of protection. She had left him unofficially many times before, only to return on a wave of pathological optimism to the criticism and violence she hated but knew so well and felt at home with.

In late May, she came to see me. "Look. Can you see a difference?" she asked. I noticed her smile and the two cups of coffee she carried (one for me). Then I realized what was different. She was wearing a short-sleeved T-shirt, and her arms were smooth and clear, free from bruises or welts. She had raised her emotional set point and was determined never again to suffer at someone else's hand. Once a set point is raised, there is no going back.

Just imagine how many unfinished novels would be published, cars taken off blocks and repaired, basements organized, and former friends contacted if people were not so used to feeling critical of themselves and ashamed for not doing what they believe is right. It is such a confidence builder to face up to our self-defeating habits and feelings and to leave them behind.

At first, this is difficult because of your fixed self-image. If you step outside this subjective framework, you will probably feel anxious. An inner voice will demand, "Who do you think you are?" Every time you counter this automatic emotional habit, you weaken your old perception of yourself and bring yourself back to a state of calm, mature confidence. Expect setbacks to follow successes, for this is new territory and the brain is fearful and wary, and will try to rush you "home." Be careful not to blow your achievement, as so many do, by making an emotional decision that will drag you back to your old familiar feelings.

Setbacks are healed with a steady application of comfort—and soon, calm prevails. The confident life is simpler. Free from the immature feelings that once clouded judgment, you'll begin to welcome the present and the future, instead of fearing them. As you grow in confidence, your retrained brain becomes more forward-thinking. It will not easily remember how you once felt. There is no greater relief than to be free to be oneself; to act in ways you believe to be right; and to truly fulfill the potential you were born with.

It will soon be time for us to part company. There is a sense of sadness in me as I write the last few words of this (for me) enormous undertaking, written in evenings, on weekends, and during vacations from my full-time work. But before I go, I will ask you for two things more.

First, I ask you to commit yourself to continuing your work on managing your feelings and living a life in which empathy and understanding replace criticism and hostility. With dedication you can replace the habits of a lifetime with new hope and enthusiasm, and walk the confident road. Richard has a wise saying I would like to pass on: "Anything you choose to do, do cheerfully." So, be cheerful as you do the work your family could not finish—developing complete confidence.

What might have been never will be. Security is yours to provide. Comfort your painful feelings. Do what is right for you, no matter how much your feelings tempt you otherwise. In these ways, you will grow in confidence.

My second request is to please keep this book handy. For now I must hand it to you. When you read it, take from it what you need. It took me many years before I could write in books and mark them up—I would feel too ashamed to do it. But I encourage you to write in this book and mark it up to make it your personal guide to confidence. Note the pages that relate especially to you and return to them. Keep the book in your kitchen, your car, or your desk drawer until you find that you automatically comfort yourself. Then you can put this book on a shelf somewhere to gather dust, for like the emotional habits of the past, you will no longer need it.

Then, you will have mastered the setbacks, calmed and comforted the feelings, and trained yourself to walk on in confidence, freed up to appreciate the world, especially its daily small joys. For me, these include the bowl of porridge (warm oatmeal with yogurt and maple syrup) my husband made for me, and the small black Labrador puppy I ran into this morning. Now that you have confidence, you will no longer walk right through the world, troubled and unseeing.

The ability to be confident may not enable you to become a totally calm person, but confidence will mostly free you from fear and anxiety. You'll feel anxiety only as a response to a logical threat, and you will automatically respond with the Winning Hand of Comfort, thus freeing yourself emotionally to make mature, independent, rational decisions about how to handle the situation. You will not be a leaner, but the one on whom others can lean.

I have total confidence that you can succeed. I have seen others do it. I do not believe that one should ever terminate a relationship unless it is destructive, so I thank you and respect your staying with me and facing yourself, which is not easy. It is difficult, but worth it. Keep the door open and your confidence will flood in.

I can imagine myself holding your Winning Hand for the very last time.

ACKNOWLEDGMENTS

When I began to write this book, I thought all I needed was a lined notebook, an automatic lead pencil, and an art gum eraser. Now at the end, I know that it takes a lot of input from others to move a manuscript from inspiration to publication. Let me tell you who helped me and how—to all of them I give great thanks:

Richard Wessler, my beloved and modest husband, wants only to be acknowledged for his typing of the manuscript.

Carol Tannenhauser, a talented writer, read every word of this book from its inception. She wisely held my feet to the fire when my words made perfect sense to me and no sense to her.

Maureen Coveney, my secretary for twenty years, is also my cheerleader. Her undying belief in this book was a light in dark moments.

Katie O'Neill, my agent, insisted that she represent this book. Her total enthusiasm and kick-ass determination is an author's dream come true.

Aliza Fogelson, my editor at ReganBooks, really "gets it." She taught me that a book needs flow and clarity.

Judith Regan, my publisher, had confidence in me. It is a joy to spend time in her company.

INDEX